HOCKEY'S
Greatest Stars

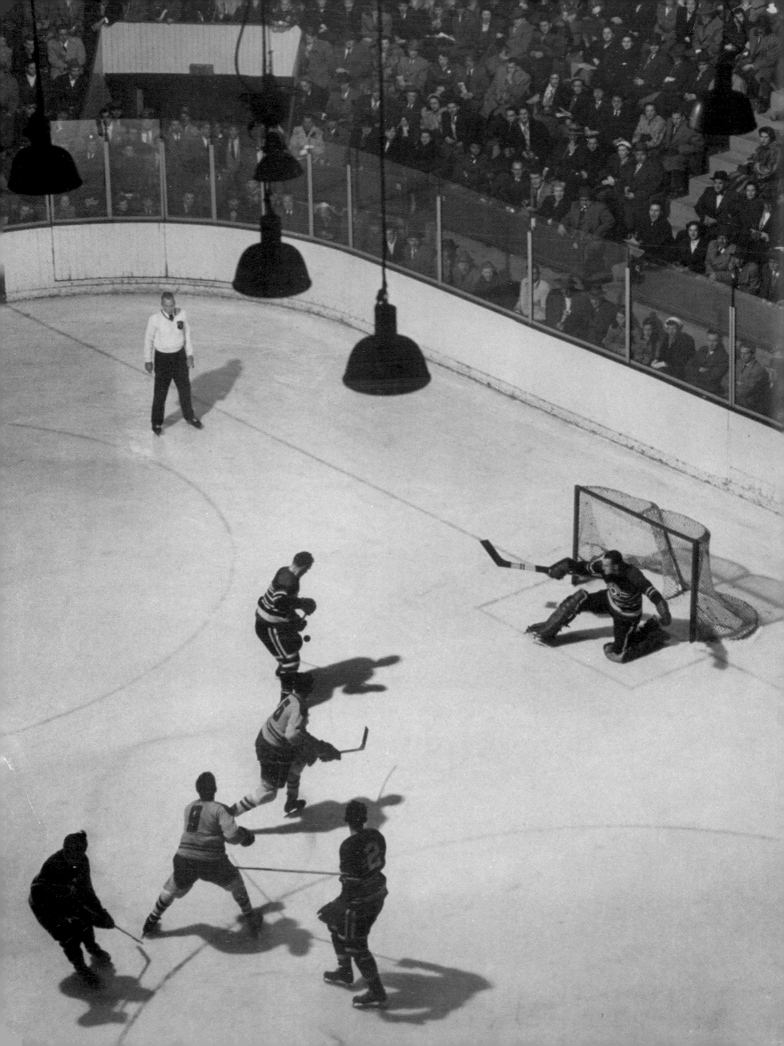

HOCKEY'S
Greatest Stars
Legends and Young Lions

Chris McDonell

FIREFLY BOOKS

A FIREFLY BOOK

Published by Firefly Books Ltd. 2005

First printing

Publisher Cataloging-in-Publication Data (U.S.)
McDonell, Chris.
    Hockey's greatest stars : legends and young lions / Chris McDonell.
2nd ed.
[192] p. : ports. (some col.) ; 32 cm.
Includes bibliographical references and index.
Summary: Profiles of hockey's greatest players ever, as well as today's most promising young players.
ISBN 1-55407-038-4 (pbk.)
1. Hockey players -- Biography. 2. National Hockey League. I. Title.
796.962/092/2 B dc22 GV848.5.A1M336 2005

Library and Archives Canada Cataloguing in Publication
McDonell, Chris
    Hockey's greatest stars : legends and young lions / Chris McDonell.
-- Rev. and updated
2nd ed.
ISBN 1-55407-038-4
    1. Hockey players--Biography. 2. National Hockey League--
Biography. I. Title.
GV848.5.A1M26 2005   796.962'092'2   C2005-901182-3

Published in the United States by
Firefly Books (U.S.) Inc.
P.O. Box 1338, Ellicott Stations
Buffalo, New York 14205

Published in Canada by
Firefly Books Ltd.
66 Leek Crescent
Richmond Hill, Ontario L4B 1H1

Cover and interior design by Tinge Design Studio

Printed in China

The publisher gratefully acknowledges the financial support for our publishing program by the Canada Council for the Arts, the Ontario Arts Council and the Government of Canada through the Book Publishing Industry Development Program.

To Sue Gordon and Isaac, Tara and Quinn McDonell-Gordon, with love and appreciation.

ACKNOWLEDGMENTS

The idea behind *Hockey's Greatest Stars: Legends and Young Lions* evolved from conversations with Lionel Koffler and Michael Worek of Firefly Books, and their colleague Brad Wilson subsequently steered this volume to completion.

Larry Scanlan was of immense help in shaping my original manuscript, as were Tracy Read and Susan Dickinson of Bookmakers Press. Joanne Richter has also put her keen editorial eye to work for me. Any errors that may remain are mine alone, for the book has been significantly strengthened by her efforts. Glenn Levy of Getty Images was a great help in sifting through an immense catalogue of images. Craig Campbell of the Hockey Hall of Fame also provided us with some rare and fabulous archival photographs.

My family continues to be a big support, in particular, my parents. My siblings, their spouses and their children also have given me encouragement, as has the smaller (but almost as loud) Gordon clan. Friends, in particular Lois and Mark Williams, Mel and Doug North, Steve Scanlan, Roy Mantle and Dave Lindsay have also been a concrete help and an appreciated sounding board.

The people I share daily life with have been the most important. My oldest son Quinn keeps me laughing, my daughter Tara's passion for the game knows no bounds, and my younger son Isaac's enthusiasm for both ice hockey and road hockey takes me to the rink. Last, Sue Gordon—my lover, my partner, my soul mate—deserves the biggest thanks.

CONTENTS

INTRODUCTION   9

THE CENTERS   13

THE WINGERS   57

THE DEFENSEMEN   101

THE GOALTENDERS   145

NOTES ON THE PHOTOGRAPHS   188

BIBLIOGRAPHY   189

INDEX   191

Introduction

"I respected 'Rocket' Richard," Gordie Howe once said, "but I didn't like him. He was the man who led the way for the rest of us. He was my pacemaker—first for career points, then for career goals. Like I tell all of the kids, if you really want to learn the game of hockey, pick somebody you admire and emulate him. I picked 'The Rocket,' and he showed me a lot."

Howe, in turn, inspired another legend. "Growing up, my player role model was always Gordie," Wayne Gretzky has said, and "The Great One" himself fired the dreams of countless future National Hockey League stars.

In the same way, every hockey fan has a favorite player or two. This has always been true, but never more so than today. Fan loyalty to a team is harder to maintain in this day of labor disagreements, franchise moves and free agency. Longtime devotees and new converts may find their personal heroes in the following pages, but popularity was not a factor for inclusion. *Hockey's Greatest Stars* comprises two groupings: the "legends," the greatest players of all time; and the "young lions," players who currently prowl NHL arenas. "Young" is a relative term, but for the purposes of this book, it means those born in 1979 or later. At the time of publication, the young players had not yet reached their twenty-sixth birthdays.

Compiling these two lists has been an arduous task. I consulted with various hockey sages, who were promised anonymity, and closely studied other lists, but nothing resembling a consensus ever resulted. The enjoyable debate lost some of its pleasure when it came time to limit the many worthy candidates to the prescribed numbers: 60 of the best ever and the top 20 young players. By organizing these lists according to position, however, certain names simply fell into place. At center, Gretzky; on wing, Howe; on defense, Bobby Orr; and in goal, Terry Sawchuk: their achievements made them automatic and unarguable choices. Corresponding young stars such as Vincent Lecavalier, Ilya Kovalchuk, Barret Jackman and Roberto Luongo were equally easy to include. Not every choice was so obvious, though.

The number-one criterion for inclusion in *Hockey's Greatest Stars* was a player's personal accomplishment. Looking at statistics and accumulated awards was instructive, but it was not enough.

Once asked what he liked best about Mario Lemieux, Howe quipped, "His paycheck." But more than player salaries have changed over the years. Statistics from different eras cannot be compared in a completely straight-forward manner. A second assist was rarely given on goals during Charlie Conacher's career in the 1930s; Georges Vezina, who died in 1926 and for whom the NHL's best goaltender award is named, never played a game in which the rules permitted a netminder to hold or smother the puck. It is an oft-repeated maxim that the best players would star in any era; yet as Nels Stewart allowed, even the renowned Howie Morenz would have had a difficult time in the NHL of the 1950s. I considered the question of how a player would fare in hockey as we now know it.

Another important ingredient in the makeup of a great hockey player is his contribution to team success. "Steve Yzerman is the best example," says winger Brendan Shanahan. "He's a guy whose image has gone back and forth so many times in the organization, and now he's considered one of the greatest captains

Toronto Maple Leaf Red Kelly (left) digs the puck out of his feet while being pursued by Montreal Canadiens Bernie "Boom Boom" Geoffrion (5) and Jean Beliveau (4). All three players eventually entered the Hockey Hall of Fame.

Boston Bruins' young center Joe Thornton challenges Montreal Canadiens goaltender Jose Theodore in 2004 playoff action.

to ever play. That's what winning does for all of us." Strong performance under playoff pressure lifted more than one player into *Hockey's Greatest Stars*, although the lack of a Stanley Cup ring was never a reason for exclusion.

"I have been able to maintain my scoring pace while guys like Guy Lafleur have tailed off," Marcel Dionne once remarked with a wistful smile. "I always get an extra two months of rest because we never make the playoffs." Among the legends in these pages are some who never hoisted the Cup—goaltender Vladislav Tretiak didn't even compete in the NHL—and the young stars who have played on Stanley Cup winners are the exception rather than the rule.

Consistency and durability were given more weight than meteoric exploits for the legends' roster, less so for the young lions. Thus, a player such as 700-goal scorer Mike Gartner is included, although he was never selected to an end-of-season All-Star Team, while 1972 Team Canada hero Paul Henderson did not make the cut. Several other players might have joined Gartner in this book had they put in more years as consistently—winger Pavel Bure springs immediately to mind. Likewise, it was hard to exclude players such as goaltender Tony Esposito, a frequent All-Star during his lengthy Hall of Fame career with the Chicago Blackhawks. Yet when everything was factored in, center Phil is the only Esposito on this honor roll.

Beyond choosing the players, I made no attempt to rank them. In the end, it came down to singular decisions—this star or that?—and the answers were never easy.

"There will always be young hockey champions," wrote journalist Andy O'Brien in 1971. "Those of tomorrow could very well force the National Hockey League to change its name to the Global Hockey League." Considering that, when he wrote, NHL players had yet to eat the humble pie that was the 1972 Summit Series, O'Brien's prediction is eerily accurate. Hockey has evolved during this generation, as a result of not only the world's best players being drawn into the NHL but also the tremendous expansion of the league. In winnowing down the lists for *Hockey's Greatest Stars*, I have tried to avoid sentimentality yet do justice to the athletes of yesteryear.

"One of the greatest parts of our game is the history," observed Gretzky at the 1999 All-Star Game. "I mean the Stanley Cup itself, the 'Original Six' teams and the star players who created the NHL." He chatted with Maurice Richard, who unveiled the new Richard Trophy for the league's top goal scorer. "There are some guys who don't get as much recognition as they deserve for getting hockey to the level it is today," he continued. "I was telling Rocket at center ice that the NHL was lucky to have him in the game."

As William Shakespeare once wrote, though, "What's past is prologue." While Richard's appearances provide a tangible link with a bygone era, so too did the veteran and now retired Gretzky, as will, eventually, the young lions profiled here. These vignettes, although arranged by position rather than in chronological order, collectively serve as a snapshot of glorious hockey history—past, present and future.

The results of my difficult decisions are now before you. After perusing the table of contents, try to put aside your own arguments for a while. The portraits offered here, in words and pictures, sketch talented, gritty and inspiring men who represent all that is wonderful and exciting about the fabulous sport of hockey. The game itself has its own charm, but the players bring it to life. Enjoy their stories and the recollection of their exploits. And watch the greatest stars still playing. Game by game, new chapters continue to be written.

The Centers

The Centers

Hockey's greatest players can be found at every position, but a team's best player is most often found at center. As the name implies, much of the game revolves around the centerman. At the opening face-off and after every stop in the action, two centers square off head-to-head. How they handle that play dictates the ensuing flow of the game. A strong face-off artist can give his team a tremendous advantage.

The drop of the puck, however, is only the beginning. A center's skills must be more varied than those of any other player. Legendary goal scorers such as Nels "Old Poison" Stewart and "Super Mario" Lemieux spent most of their careers leaving defensive responsibilities to others, but a star such as Steve Yzerman has a place in this book in part because of his evolution from an offensive dynamo into a two-way player. With rare exceptions, the centerman must be skilled both on the attack—passing and shooting—and in checking.

The centers featured here include slightly built men such as Marcel Dionne and Henri Richard as well as behemoths like Joe Thornton and Phil Esposito. "Scoring is easy," said Esposito, whom most defensemen found immovable. "You stand in the slot, take your beating and shoot the puck in the net." At the opposite extreme, Richard speaks about using his diminutive size to scoot under a defenseman's reach and get in alone on the goalie.

But the greatest center of all time is physically unremarkable in any way. The 6-foot, 175-pound Wayne Gretzky is arguably the greatest player ever to have laced on skates, yet myriad others have possessed a stronger shot, greater speed and superior strength. Appropriately, another sense of the word "center" means "to concentrate and focus," and it is in this area that Gretzky proved to be without peer. Unique in his ability to "read" a play and dissect the possibilities, he regularly surprised everyone by executing the unexpected but clearly best option.

Obviously, there are different ways to approach the position, but it is no coincidence that most of the centers profiled in this book have served as team captain. Exceptional physical skills alone do not make an elite center. Brawn is an obvious asset, but the savvy of Stan Mikita, the fortitude of the diabetic Bobby Clarke and the ambassadorial presence of Jean Beliveau are traits that all of these centers possess to a high degree. As critical to their teams' success as are their prodigious talents, leadership is also a key ingredient.

Strength up the middle is a general prerequisite for a championship team. "The measure of Mark Messier's game is not in goals and assists," observed Gretzky. "The statistic he cares about is 'number of Stanley Cups won.'" But while Hall of Fame member Dionne didn't win a single title, he remains, 15 years after retiring, among the top five in NHL history in both career goals and points scored. Stanley Cup rings are not essential components of greatness, as some of the young centers featured here may eventually discover. To date, only Vincent Lecavalier has sipped champagne from the Cup, but an unquenchable thirst for victory is characteristic of every center in this book.

LEGENDS

Syl Apps

Jean Beliveau

Bobby Clarke

Marcel Dionne

Phil Esposito

Wayne Gretzky

Mario Lemieux

Mark Messier

Stan Mikita

Howie Morenz

Henri Richard

Milt Schmidt

Nels Stewart

Bryan Trottier

Steve Yzerman

YOUNG LIONS

Mike Comrie

Scott Gomez

Vincent Lecavalier

Jason Spezza

Joe Thornton

Opposite: New Jersey Devil Scott Gomez celebrates his team's 2003 Stanley Cup victory. Previous page: In a classic match-up, budding superstar Wayne Gretzky faces off against fellow center Bryan Trottier.

Syl Apps

Syl Apps combined Boy Scout virtue with exceptional athletic ability—the perfect profile for a hockey hero. Although Apps had only a 10-season career, he is still regarded as the greatest captain the Toronto Maple Leafs ever had. His minuscule 56 career penalty minutes attest to his sportsmanship, but his chiseled good looks, great physical strength and slick stickhandling, passing and scoring were equally important to the lasting image he created.

Apps helped the Maple Leafs win three Stanley Cups, captained the team after his World War II service and quit the game while still at his peak. An all-round athlete who excelled at hockey, football and track, Apps was the 1934 Commonwealth Games pole vault champion and delayed accepting Conn Smythe's invitation to join the Maple Leafs so that he could compete in the 1936 Olympics.

He went on to win the inaugural Calder Trophy in 1937, but the spring of 1942 provided his greatest excitement. "Nothing can compare," he said, "with the thrill of winning our fourth in a row over the Red Wings after they had won three straight." No other team has ever made such an amazing comeback in the Stanley Cup finals. "If you want to pin me down to not only my biggest night in hockey but also my biggest second," he told writer Trent Frayne in 1949, "I'll say it was the last tick of the clock that sounded the final bell. I'll never forget it."

Halfway through the 1942–43 season, Apps broke his leg and shocked owner Conn Smythe when he tried to return part of his salary—he felt he hadn't earned his full pay. Once the leg healed, he volunteered for Canadian military service, missing two full NHL seasons at the height of his career.

"When he hits the defense," said Quackenbush, "he doesn't slow down, he digs in."

Apps picked up right where he had left off. In 1947, Hall of Fame defenseman Bill Quackenbush claimed that Apps was the hardest player in the league to stop. "When he hits the defense," said Quackenbush, "he doesn't slow down, he digs in. That extra burst of speed makes him awful tough." Apps, however, believed he had lost a step. He wanted to retire before he "slowed the team down," but he set one last target: 200 career goals.

Heading into the final weekend of play in the spring of 1948, Apps needed only three more goals to reach 200. He scored one on Saturday night. In Sunday's game against Detroit, he banged in another one after a goal-mouth scramble in the second period. Later in the same period, Harry Watson of the Leafs had an excellent scoring opportunity, but instead of shooting, he passed to Apps, who scored goal 200. "I just blasted it with everything I had," said Apps. Apps put the icing on the cake by completing a hat trick in the third period.

The press commented on how generous Watson had been in setting Apps up for the goal. "It was nice of him all right," agreed Apps, "but you should have heard the yelling I was doing at him to pass it!" Apps hoisted the Stanley Cup for the second consecutive year, but when the Leafs "three-peated" the following season, it was without Apps in the lineup. The 33-year-old captain had retired and joined the business world.

"I was always keen about politics," explained Apps, when he answered yet another calling years later. He was elected as a member of the governing Progressive Conservative Party in 1963, and his image was untarnished by 11 years in Ontario politics. True to form, he retired on his own terms in 1974.

DATE OF BIRTH
Paris, Ontario
January 18, 1915–December 24, 1998

NHL CAREER
1936–43, 1945–8
Toronto

	GP	G	A	TP	PIM
RS	423	201	231	432	56
PO	69	25	28	53	16

AWARDS
1st All-Star (2), 2nd All-Star (3), Calder,
Stanley Cup (3), HOF 1961

Jean Beliveau

No one meeting Jean Beliveau today would be surprised to hear that he was offered an appointment to the Canadian Senate as well as the prestigious position of Governor General of Canada. And during his 20-year NHL hockey career, Beliveau was every bit as much the diplomat. Although he was never a recipient of the Lady Byng Trophy, Beliveau was hockey's greatest gentleman and a born leader. Upon Maurice "Rocket" Richard's retirement from the Montreal Canadiens in 1960, Beliveau quickly became the quintessential team captain.

James Christie of *The Globe and Mail* recorded Beliveau's own reflections on leadership: "To me, there are three things that a captain should do. First is what the fans see during a game. There is your play and the job you do as the man in the middle, the man between the coaches and the players and the referee. Second, there is the job every day in the dressing room. You have to listen to your teammates, even help them with their personal problems. I always tried to solve things right there in the dressing room, without going to management. Third, especially with the Canadiens, you act as a spokesman and representative wherever you go. But the most important of these is number two. You have to be ready to give time to your teammates in any situation." Both on and off the ice, "Le Gros Bill" earned undying respect.

"You have to be ready to give time to your teammates in any situation."

Few players have entered the NHL with as much fanfare as did Beliveau. The Canadiens wooed him unsuccessfully for years. Beliveau's patience paid off: By the time he signed with Montreal at age 22, he was one of the highest-paid players in the NHL. His first contract paid $105,000 over five years, plus bonuses—an astronomical sum in 1953. But Beliveau had been making similar money with the Quebec Aces in the Quebec Hockey League, and it took more than cash to get him into the NHL.

Beliveau played as a junior for two years in Quebec City with the Citadels and was honored with his first "Jean Beliveau Night" in 1951. The whole city had embraced the 61-goal scorer (in a 43-game season). Although Montreal beckoned, Beliveau decided to stay in Quebec City. In an ostensibly amateur league, Beliveau earned a then-enormous $15,000 a year, and he reciprocated with 45- and 50-goal seasons. Meanwhile, he had already signed a contract with Montreal stipulating that he would play for the Canadiens when he turned professional.

Beliveau had played two NHL games in 1950–51, getting a goal and an assist, and he donned the famous *bleu, blanc et rouge* sweater for three games in the 1952–53 season, scoring five times. The Canadiens took drastic action: They bought the entire Quebec senior league and made it officially professional. Beliveau's hand was forced, and at the start of the 1953–54 season, he began his much-anticipated rookie campaign.

Unfortunately, Beliveau struggled at the outset, was injured and finished with an unimpressive 13 goals and 21 assists in 44 games. Montreal's perseverance was rewarded in his second season (37 goals, 36 assists); in the third season, even more so. "I used to wonder why 'Rocket' Richard would blow up when other players chopped at him," Beliveau said in 1956, "but I am beginning to understand." Responding to critics who urged him to use his size and strength to better advantage, Beliveau adopted a more belligerent style, albeit temporarily. His 143 penalty minutes in 1955–56 set a team record, but more important, his 47 goals and 41 assists led the league. He scored 12 more goals in Montreal's 10-game march to Stanley Cup victory, the first of five consecutive winning seasons.

Although Beliveau failed to win another scoring title, the goals came regularly over the years. On February 11, 1971, during his final NHL season, he became only the fourth player to record 500 career goals. He capped his glorious career by hoisting the Stanley Cup for a tenth time.

DATE OF BIRTH
Trois Rivières, Quebec
August 31, 1931–

NHL CAREER
1953–71
Montreal

	GP	G	A	TP	PIM
RS	1125	507	712	1219	1029
PO	162	79	97	176	211

AWARDS

1st All-Star (6), 2nd All-Star (4), Ross, Hart (2), Smythe, Stanley Cup (10), HOF 1972

Bobby Clarke

One of hockey's greatest leaders and one of its dirtiest players, Bobby Clarke earned both tags. Each characterization was intrinsic to Clarke's role in the 1970s as captain of Philadelphia's infamous "Broad Street Bullies," a team that constantly tried to blur the line between aggression and violence. Red Kelly, then coach of the Toronto Maple Leafs, added an important nuance: "I don't think I'd call Clarke dirty—mean is a better word."

"Guys who complain about my being dirty," countered Clarke, "should go home with my body at night. I've eaten quite a few too"—sticks, that is. Clarke's toothless grin has become one of hockey's enduring images, and it is still used to sell beer and the game thirty years after he led Philadelphia to its first of two consecutive Stanley Cups in 1974.

"I don't think I'd call Clarke dirty— mean is a better word."

Clarke showed early promise as a hockey player in Flin Flon, Manitoba, but at the age of 15, he'd arrived at a crossroads. Diagnosed with juvenile diabetes, Clarke began self-administering the daily insulin injections necessary to stay alive. Medical advice confirmed his conviction that his diabetes need not end his dream of playing professional hockey, and by the time Clarke was 17, he was starring for the Flin Flon Bombers in the junior Western Hockey League. Working in the mines a few hours each day further hardened his resolve to make hockey his career.

Clarke entered the 1969 NHL entry draft ranked the premier player in the WHL, but many questioned whether he could sustain the NHL pace. The Philadelphia Flyers took a chance on him with their second pick, seventeenth overall. It was the best move the franchise ever made.

Clarke fainted after his first shift in training camp, but it was soon determined that his diet simply needed to be adjusted, and he had a decent 1969–70 rookie season. His growing success and perseverance were acknowledged when he won the Bill Masterton Trophy in 1972. Later that fall, Clarke played a big role in Team Canada's narrow victory over the Soviet Union. His tenacious checking was invaluable, but Clarke's vicious two-handed slash on the ankle of Soviet star Valeri Kharlamov is what is best remembered. The intentional foul, took Kharlamov out of the critical last three games of the series. "It's not something I'm really proud of," Clarke recently noted, "but I honestly can't say I was ashamed to do it."

"Clarke is our leader," noted Flyers' goalie Bernie Parent. "He works so hard himself that the other guys just have to work to keep up. He is the guy who makes us go." Clarke was indeed visibly industrious, with his head bobbing as he raced about the ice, but he was also a gifted player. He danced with the puck and threaded slick passes to his teammates. Yet there were games when Clarke did seem to dig deeper than humanly possible, dragging his team up by the bootstraps to victory, particularly in the 1974 Stanley Cup finals.

Facing the powerful Boston Bruins, Clarke's Flyers were down 2-0 in game two after losing the series opener. Clarke scored once to narrow Boston's lead, then tied the game with only 52 seconds left in regulation time. With 12 minutes gone in overtime, Clarke concluded a magnificent evening's work by completing a hat trick. The Bruins never fully recovered, and Clarke delivered the *coup de grâce* to Boston's hopes when he lured Bobby Orr into hauling him down with just over two minutes remaining in the deciding game. With Orr sitting in the penalty box, the Flyers won the game 1-0 and hoisted the Stanley Cup for the first time.

Clarke is well into his second term as Philadelphia's general manager. Using the same approach to model his club that was so successful to him as a player, he has consistently constructed big and tough Stanley Cup contenders.

DATE OF BIRTH
Flin Flon, Manitoba
August 13, 1949–

NHL CAREER
1969–84
Philadelphia

	GP	G	A	TP	PIM	AWARDS
RS	1144	358	852	1210	1433	1st All-Star (2), 2nd All-Star (2), Hart (3), Pearson,
PO	136	42	77	119	152	Masterton, Stanley Cup (2), HOF 1987

Marcel Dionne

On skates, he was as solid as a fire hydrant and not much bigger, but Marcel Dionne had quick acceleration and an aggressive run-and-gun style that put him in the spotlight at a young age. Family and hometown pressures in Quebec were so great during his teenage years that the scoring sensation opted to play in Ontario's junior league, where, in spite of the culture shock he experienced, he won two consecutive scoring championships.

Dionne stood just under five-foot-eight, but NHL scouts ranked him with Guy Lafleur, his perennial rival in Quebec. After some dithering, the Montreal Canadiens selected Lafleur as the number-one pick in the 1971 NHL entry draft, and the Detroit Red Wings quickly snapped up Dionne with the second pick.

Dionne had an auspicious rookie year, with 28 goals and 49 assists, but his team was in turmoil. Problems at the top of the Red Wings organization trickled down to the players. Dionne was suspended from the team twice for arguing with his coach. "You have to find a way to survive," maintained Dionne. He racked up 366 points in four seasons with the Wings and moved into the top tier of the league's scoring race, finishing behind Bobby Orr and Phil Esposito in the 1974–75 season. But Dionne and the Red Wings never got a hint of playoff action together.

"My heart is still with the Kings, but my body is with the Rangers."

Discouraged by the losing atmosphere in the Motor City, Dionne became the first high-profile player to test the new free-agent market. In 1975, the Los Angeles Kings made a generous offer, and Dionne jumped at the chance to play for a team that had been rising consistently in the standings. Unfortunately, Dionne soon found himself in a familiar situation. While the Kings enjoyed little success during the almost 12 seasons he spent in Los Angeles, Dionne remained an offensive force. In his second season in L.A.'s purple and gold, he broke the 50-goal plateau for the first of six times in seven years.

His clean play twice earned him the Lady Byng Trophy; he also won the Art Ross Trophy, by the narrowest of margins. Dionne had to come up with two assists in the final game of the 1979–80 campaign to match Gretzky's late-season surge to 137 points. Dionne got the title, with 53 goals versus Gretzky's 51.

Dionne appreciated his trophies, but he valued none so much as the Pearson Award as the league's MVP, which he won in 1979 and 1980 based on votes by his fellow players. Dionne had lost respect for the hockey writers when they had voted him center for the First All-Star Team for the 1976–77 season. "I played the right wing in the Canada Cup that September," he explained. "I went back to Los Angeles, played the whole year at right wing, and they voted for me at center." His success that season notwithstanding, Dionne was soon back in the pivot position, where his freewheeling style gave defensemen nightmares. Dave Taylor and Charlie Simmer joined him at his flanks, and the "Triple Crown Line" quickly gathered notice as one of the NHL's best.

Ostensibly for a shot at a Stanley Cup, Dionne demanded a trade in 1986–87, although he later claimed that his request was a contract-negotiation ploy. To his dismay, he became a New York Ranger. "My heart is still with the Kings," the outspoken star admitted with controversial candor two weeks later, "but my body is with the Rangers."

Dionne moved into third place in career goals scored, but as his always-churning legs started to slow, the goals came further and further apart. "Because you love the game so much," said Dionne, "you think it will never end." He spent nine games in the minors before retiring in 1989.

DATE OF BIRTH
Drummondville, Quebec
August 3, 1951–

NHL CAREER
1971–89
Detroit, Los Angeles, NY Rangers

	GP	G	A	TP	PIM	AWARDS
RS	1384	731	1040	1771	600	1st All-Star (2), 2nd All-Star (2), Ross,
PO	49	21	24	45	17	Byng (2), Pearson (2), HOF 1992

Phil Esposito

Phil Esposito was blessed with many skills as a hockey player, but it was his passion that set him apart. He shattered the single-season scoring record, won five scoring championships and helped lead his team to two Stanley Cup victories. Yet his emotional nature had its greatest impact at the midpoint of the historic 1972 Summit Series.

The roundly favored Canadians had just suffered their second defeat to the Soviets, concluding their home half of the series with a win, a tie and two losses. An angry Vancouver crowd booed Team Canada. "We gave it our best," scolded an obviously exhausted Esposito in a televised interview. "All of us guys are really disheartened.... We came out because we love Canada. And I don't think it is fair that we should be booed." Few watching were unmoved. The nation rallied behind the team, which eked out a slim and miraculous series victory. Paul Henderson's winning goals in the last three games are forever etched into the Canadian consciousness, but Esposito's leadership and effectiveness on the ice—he led the series in scoring—were arguably even more crucial.

"I don't think it is fair that we should be booed."

If Esposito had a weakness, it was his skating. But Esposito was a hulking bear of a man who became an immovable object when he parked himself in front of the net. At the age of 19, he caught on with the St. Catharines Teepees, a junior team affiliated with the Chicago Blackhawks.

Esposito served a three-year minor-league apprenticeship, and when he finally earned a permanent spot in the NHL for the 1964–65 season, it was a golden one. He centered a line with Bobby Hull on his left. With Esposito feeding him, Hull enjoyed seasons of 39, 54 and 52 goals. Esposito put the puck in the net too, although his detractors claimed many of them were "garbage" goals, a charge he faced throughout his career.

"Espo" was sent to the Boston Bruins in 1967 in one of the most lopsided trades in NHL history. He joined Ken Hodge and Fred Stanfield in Boston, while Pit Martin, Gilles Marotte and goalie Jack Norris went to Chicago. Hodge and Stanfield became key elements in a powerhouse Boston club, and Esposito achieved even greater heights.

He won the Art Ross Trophy in his second season in Beantown, after finishing second to Chicago's Stan Mikita the previous year. He earned runner-up status again in 1970 (to Bobby Orr), but he erupted the next season with a 76-goal, 76-assist campaign, eclipsing Bobby Hull's 58-goal record, set the previous year. In fact, Esposito had raised the bar so high that it would be 20 years before his single-season records started falling to a young player named Wayne Gretzky.

Esposito dominated the dressing room as well as the scoring race with his gregarious manner and a penchant for superstition. His locker was festooned with good-luck charms, and he made sure that no one left hockey sticks crossed on the floor, for fear they would create bad luck.

Esposito and Orr were the linchpins of the Bruins' success and two Stanley Cup victories, but when the team began to falter in 1975, Boston's general manager Harry Sinden felt that a shake-up was needed. Esposito and Carol Vadnais went to their archrival, the New York Rangers, in return for Brad Park, Jean Ratelle and Joe Zanussi. While he never challenged for the scoring title again, Esposito won legions of fans in the Big Apple and took the Rangers to the Stanley Cup finals in 1979. He retired in 1981, second only to Gordie Howe in NHL career goals and points scored.

DATE OF BIRTH
Sault Ste. Marie, Ontario
February 20, 1942–

NHL CAREER
1963–81
Chicago, Boston, NY Rangers

	GP	G	A	TP	PIM	AWARDS
RS	1282	717	873	1590	910	1st All-Star (6), 2nd All-Star, Ross (5), Hart (2),
PO	130	61	76	137	137	Pearson (2), Stanley Cup (2), HOF 1984

Wayne Gretzky

Although everyone knew Wayne Gretzky's career would eventually end, it was a sad day for hockey when he announced his retirement at the end of the 1998–99 season. Gretzky, already owner of 61 NHL records, including almost all of the most significant scoring records, decided to hang up his skates before he slipped out of the NHL elite. Ovations and accolades followed Gretzky's final game in Madison Square Garden, and the NHL announced the most fitting tribute of all: No player on any team will ever wear Gretzky's number 99 again.

Like Abe Lincoln's log cabin in America, the Gretzky backyard rink is a part of Canadian folklore. Even as a child, Gretzky was the center of national attention: At age 10, he scored 378 goals in a 69-game season, and in 1978, at age 17, he signed his first professional contract with the Indianapolis Racers of the WHA. Gretzky's contract was soon sold to Peter Pocklington, owner of the Edmonton Oilers.

"The pace seems a little faster in this league," he commented when his team joined the NHL, "but the WHA was a good league. I feel I did well for my first year. I will do my best and hope it's good enough." A "merger" rule disqualified Gretzky from Calder Trophy voting, and he suffered further disappointment when his 51 goals and 86 assists left him tied with Marcel Dionne for total points. Dionne was awarded the scoring crown based on his 53 goals. "I was always taught that an assist is as good as a goal," stated Gretzky tersely, but for the next seven years, he beat his closest rival by an average of 66 points.

"I couldn't beat people with my strength. My eyes and my mind have to do most of the work."

"Wayne kind of sneaks up on you," Edmonton coach Glen Sather once remarked. "He doesn't have Bobby Hull's power or Bobby Orr's speed, but he has the same magic."

Orr himself was amazed. "You figure a guy has Gretzky trapped. Next thing you know, Gretzky has given the puck to somebody you figure he couldn't even see."

While admitting to often "sensing" where his teammates are, Gretzky believes his celebrated vision was honed by fear. He had always played against older, bigger, and stronger opponents. "I couldn't beat people with my strength," the slight superstar once explained. "My eyes and my mind have to do most of the work."

While his natural gifts were awesome, Gretzky had always been a hard worker. "First, you have to have a passion and a love for the sport," he declared. "Second, you have to have a dedication to it." He dominated the NHL during the regular season, most notably with his 92-goal, 120-assist 1981–82 campaign and his 52-goal 163-assist 1985–86 year, but Gretzky also enjoyed postseason success. "Kids grow up dreaming about holding up the Stanley Cup," he once said. "That dream fuels you in the playoffs." But after leading Edmonton to four Stanley Cups, "The Great One" was sold to the Los Angeles Kings in 1988.

His "trade" was seen by many Canadians as a national disaster, but his presence invigorated the L.A. franchise and stimulated NHL growth throughout the southern United States. Gretzky won three more scoring championships in Los Angeles, but he requested a trade to a contender in 1995–96. After a short stay in St. Louis, he headed for Broadway and the New York Rangers.

Post-retirement, Gretzky became part owner of the Phoenix Coyotes. He also was general manager of Team Canada, which won a 2002 Olympic gold medal and the 2004 World Cup. Although Gretzky now makes his home in California, he remains one of Canada's favorite sons.

DATE OF BIRTH
Brantford, Ontario
January 26, 1961–

NHL CAREER
1979–99
Edmonton, Los Angeles, St. Louis, NY Rangers

	GP	G	A	TP	PIM	AWARDS
RS	1487	894	1963	2857	577	1st All-Star (8), 2nd All-Star (7), Ross (10), Hart (9), Byng
PO	208	122	260	382	66	(5), Pearson (5), Smythe (2), Stanley Cup (4), HOF 1999

Mario Lemieux

Mario Lemieux scored on the first shift of his first NHL game with his first shot on net. No other player has ever made so auspicious a debut. The Pittsburgh Penguins selected Lemieux with the first pick in the 1984 NHL entry draft, refusing tempting offers for proven NHL players. The highly touted junior—he scored 282 points in his last season—stepped right into the NHL and won the Calder Trophy with his first 100-point seasons, notching 43 goals. Disbelievers accused Lemieux of neglecting his defensive responsibilities, but the Penguins were looking for offense and Lemieux delivered.

The 1985 NHL All-Star Game offered Lemieux the perfect stage to silence his critics. He scored twice and had one helper in leading his team to victory, and was named the game's MVP, an honor he would receive twice more in the next five years. Yet the Penguins continued to languish near the league's cellar.

Lemieux played brilliantly for Canada in the 1987 Canada Cup tournament, and with 168 points, dethroned Gretzky as league-scoring champion in the 1987–88 season. He retained the title with an amazing 199 points the following year. When the Penguins made the playoffs that year, Lemieux had fulfilled one of his primary goals.

"I'm not coming back to be an average player."

The team slipped in 1989–90, however, and failed to qualify for postseason action (Lemieux missed 21 games because of a herniated disk in his back but still managed to amass 123 points), and Lemieux's detractors were vocal once more.

After Lemieux's back surgery that summer, a deep infection set in, and the center missed the first 50 games of the regular season. But he came back, tallied 45 points in 26 games and almost matched that total with 16 goals and 28 assists in the playoffs. After raising the Stanley Cup in victory, he was awarded the Conn Smythe Trophy.

Lemieux punctuated that glorious achievement in 1991–92 with another scoring title and his second Conn Smythe Trophy and a Stanley Cup ring. He will be best remembered, however, for his heroics the following year.

Lemieux was diagnosed with Hodgkin's disease and underwent two months of grueling radiation treatment before rejoining the Penguins. Yet he won his fourth Art Ross Trophy by a 12-point margin. The Penguins finished atop the league, and although they failed to win the Cup again, Lemieux won his

second Hart Trophy (MVP), his third Pearson Award (players' choice for MVP) and the Bill Masterton Trophy (for his perseverance and dedication to the game).

The next season, Lemieux missed 58 games due to complications from further back surgery. Still anemic from the radiation therapy, an exhausted Lemieux sat out the entire 1994–95 season to recuperate. But he made a reassuring pronouncement: "I'm not coming back to be an average player." He proved his point by winning the scoring championship the next two seasons.

Yet Lemieux was not happy. He began to talk of retirement, citing both a desire to spend more time with his young family and a distaste for the game of clutching, hooking and grabbing that the NHL tolerated.

True to his word, the 31-year-old hung up his skates at the end of the 1996–97 season. The Hockey Hall of Fame inducted Lemieux immediately, but his playing days weren't over. When the Penguins threatened bankruptcy, Lemieux brokered a deal to keep the team afloat by taking an ownership position and returning to play in 2000–01. "Super Mario" continues to show why he will always be remembered as one of the game's most illustrious stars.

DATE OF BIRTH
Montreal, Quebec
October 5, 1965–

NHL CAREER
1984–94, 1995–97, 2000–04
Pittsburgh

	GP	G	A	TP	PIM	AWARDS
RS	889	683	1018	1701	818	1st All-Star (5), 2nd All-Star (3), Calder, Ross (6),
PO	107	76	96	172	87	Hart (3), Masterton, Pearson (4), Smythe (2),
						Stanley Cup (2), HOF 1997

Mark Messier

"I can never shrug off a defeat," Mark Messier has said. "I can remember a friend of mine—a rookie and a real competitor—on a team that hadn't done well for years. He'd be upset after a loss, and the veterans would say, 'Listen, don't worry about it. There's nothing you can do.' That's why some teams never get turned around. They accept losing." Only Messier has captained two different teams to the Stanley Cup.

Messier was 17 years old when he turned professional with the Indianapolis Racers in 1979—ironically, he was brought in to replace Wayne Gretzky, who had been sold to Edmonton. Although he scored only one goal that year, Messier was drafted by the Edmonton Oilers when the NHL swallowed the rival league that summer.

Mean, with a fierce glare, "Moose" Messier learned to use his speed and aggression to record his first and only 50-goal season in 1981–82, at the same time making the First All-Star Team. He broke the 100-point barrier the following season and had 15 playoff goals before being injured prior to the final round. Postseason success, however, was his destiny.

"I can never shrug off a defeat."

Messier was at his best when the young Oilers faced the veteran New York Islanders in the 1984 Stanley Cup finals. In the third game of the series, he scored a dramatic goal, and the Islanders didn't recover. Messier won the Conn Smythe Trophy winner as the playoffs' MVP. He continued to earn All-Star status and was a huge part of Edmonton's first four Stanley Cups, always scoring at least 25 playoff points. But it took a separation from Gretzky to bring Messier to his highest heights.

Messier became Edmonton's captain in 1988, when Gretzky was sold to the Los Angeles Kings. He hit a career high with 129 points in 1989–90 and won both the Hart Trophy and the Pearson Award. Messier then led all playoff scorers by contributing 22 assists toward Edmonton's fifth Stanley Cup win. "I don't think we could have pulled it off without Mark," said teammate Craig Simpson. "He held us all together."

Continuing to sell off its assets, Edmonton sent Messier to the Rangers just before the 1991–92 season got under way. He stormed Manhattan and earned the Hart Trophy and the Pearson Award again. "The players talk about what it would be like to skate around Madison Square Garden with the Cup," said Messier, not one to rest on his laurels. "And we talk about what it would be like to have a parade down Broadway. You've got to visualize these things if you want to make them happen." After a disappointing 1992–93 season, Messier took a great risk in the 1994 playoffs. Down three games to two against New Jersey in the semifinals, Messier offered a guarantee. "We know we are going to go in there and win Game Six and bring it back to the Garden," he announced. The Rangers had their backs tightly against the wall, trailing 2-1 after two periods, before Messier took over and notched a third-period hat trick to secure the game. The Rangers prevailed in Game Seven and against Vancouver in the finals, and Messier has his sixth Cup ring.

"There aren't any motives for me other than wanting to compete and win," said free-agent Messier when he signed a five-year contract with the Canucks in 1997. "It begins and ends with that." Vancouver fans were hopeful that the legendary "Greatest Leader in NHL History" would lead their team to the promised land, but it wasn't to be. After three disappointing seasons, Messier rejoined the Rangers. Although Messier has moved into second place all-time in career points, the Rangers have floundered. "When I hear that legend talk, I actually feel a little guilty, a little embarrassed," remarked Messier. "One player, no matter how good a leader on and off the ice, does not win the Stanley Cup. Your teammates have to have the same burning desire as you."

DATE OF BIRTH
Edmonton, Alberta
January 18, 1961–

NHL CAREER
1979–2004
Edmonton, NY Rangers, Vancouver

	GP	G	A	TP	PIM	AWARDS
RS	1756	694	1193	1887	1910	1st All-Star (4), 2nd All-Star, Hart (2),
PO	236	109	186	295	244	Pearson (2), Smythe, Stanley Cup (6)

Stan Mikita

Many of the meanest men on ice turn into the most kindly once they step off it. But Stan Mikita took that character transformation in a different direction. The once-chippy, frequently penalized scoring whiz drastically reduced his time in the penalty box while remaining the league's top playmaker. He was awarded the Lady Byng Trophy (most gentlemanly player), the Art Ross Trophy (most scoring points) and the Hart Trophy (most valuable player) at the end of the 1966–67 *and* 1967–68 seasons. No one else has ever won that triumvirate of awards in one season, let alone two.

On May 20, 1940, Mikita was born Stanislav Guoth in Sokolce, Czechoslovakia. Reflecting on their poverty and uncertain future, his parents decided in 1948 that it would be in their son's best interest to join his aunt and uncle, who had immigrated to Canada. The Mikitas of St. Catharines, Ontario, adopted Stan as their son, and he soon discovered hockey.

He excelled at the game, and hockey allowed him to avenge the taunts he faced because of his strongly accented English. "I wasn't going to be pushed around or laughed at," Mikita explained. "That egged me on, made me perform better. I said I was going to be better than those guys." Small but fiery, Mikita carried a chip on his shoulder for years.

"He was tricky, a good stickhandler and one of the best face-off men in the business."

That all changed when Mikita married and became a father. Asked by his young daughter why he had to sit by himself so often (in the penalty box), Mikita was embarrassed by his own answer. He determined to curb his anger and work harder, while sacrificing nothing on the score sheet.

Mikita won only one Stanley Cup, in 1961, and he led all playoff scorers that season. His most productive years were still to come, though, and the "Scooter Line" (Mikita between Doug Mohns and Ken Wharram) gave opposition goalies trouble for five years in the 1960s. Red Kelly, who faced Mikita on defense, at center and behind the bench, paid tribute when he stated: "Mikita would fool you, because he could always pull something extra out of the hat. He was tricky, a good stickhandler and one of the best face-off men in the business."

Mikita's constant tinkering led to his accidental discovery of the benefits of the curved stick in 1961. He noticed how the puck behaved unpredictably when he fired a shot in frustration with a stick blade cracked into a severe hook. After further experimentation, the "banana blade" was born—and eventually banned. Mikita was also one of the first players to wear a helmet as a preventive measure. Soon, his own improved helmet design was on the market.

Despite Mikita's many achievements, he remained in the shadow of his teammate Bobby Hull for most of his long career. Mikita and Hull first played together in high school, then in junior hockey and finally with the Chicago Blackhawks. Hull's explosive power and beaming smile contrasted sharply with Mikita's sometimes abrasive personality, acerbic wit and use of finesse over brawn. Mikita, who always denied resenting Hull, once explained, "I played hard and got the job done. But I didn't lift fans out of their seats doing it, and Bobby did."

Still, when he scored his 500th career goal in Chicago Stadium on February 27, 1977, the crowd's roar was ear-splitting. Mikita's number 21 was officially retired by the Blackhawks the season after he hung up his skates—he was the first player to be so honored in that franchise's history. And fittingly, Hull and Mikita entered the Hockey Hall of Fame together in 1983.

DATE OF BIRTH
Sokolce, Czechoslovakia
May 20, 1940–

NHL CAREER
1958–80
Chicago

	GP	G	A	TP	PIM	AWARDS
RS	1394	541	926	1467	1270	1st All-Star (6), 2nd All-Star (2), Ross (4),
PO	155	59	91	150	169	Hart (2), Byng (2), Stanley Cup, HOF 1983

Howie Morenz

It was a funeral unlike any seen before in Canada. On March 11, 1937, Howie Morenz's body lay in state at center ice in the Montreal Forum. In three hours, more than 50,000 mourners filed past Morenz's casket. An estimated 250,000 people lined the route of his funeral procession. Hockey had lost one of its greatest stars.

Morenz earned the nickname of "Mitchell Meteor" with his hometown Mitchell Juveniles. Morenz's next team, in nearby Stratford, won a provincial title in 1921, and the "Stratford Streak" caught the attention of the Montreal Canadiens.

After reluctantly agreeing to play for Montreal two years later, a homesick Morenz tried to break his contract and headed back to Mitchell during his first training camp. Cecil Hart of the Canadiens went after him, and when he placed $850 cash—Morenz's signing bonus—on the kitchen table, he convinced the whole Morenz family that Howie should return to Montreal.

Morenz quickly became famous for his blazing rushes and reckless style of hockey. Seemingly able to accelerate to top speed in a single stride, he helped establish Montreal's growing reputation for "fire wagon" hockey. By the end of his rookie NHL year of 1923–24, Morenz had tied for eighth in league scoring and had helped Montreal win its first Stanley Cup since 1916. Morenz eventually won two scoring crowns and was named the most-valuable player in the league three times.

"His shot was just like a bullet."

"He could adjust to any situation," recalled King Clancy in 1964. "He could barge between a defense, or he could poke a puck between your legs, then wheel around you and pick it up. His shot was just like a bullet, and he didn't fool around looking for an opening, he just let it go."

In his second NHL season, in a game against the New York Rangers, Morenz knocked out four of Bun Cook's front teeth with the butt end of his stick while digging for the puck. Morenz immediately dropped his stick and helped Cook off the ice. "It was just an accident," explained Cook after the game. "Howie wouldn't pull anything like that intentionally."

Cook's feelings were later echoed by Boston's notorious Eddie Shore. "Everybody likes Howie," said Shore. "He's the one player who doesn't deserve any rough treatment."

Yet years of success and admiration didn't stop the Canadiens from trading Morenz to the Chicago Blackhawks in the summer of 1934. He had started to slow down the previous season. Leo

Dandurand, general manager of the Canadiens, lent a little dignity to the situation when he retired Morenz's number 7. Morenz sadly accepted his fate, but he hated Chicago. Halfway through his second mediocre season with the Blackhawks, he was traded again, this time to the New York Rangers. He finished out the 1935–36 season as a Ranger, but when his old admirer Cecil Hart was installed as Montreal's new general manager that summer, Morenz became a Hab again.

His return to Montreal seemed to be a tonic for Morenz, and he began to show signs of his old magic. Then tragedy struck. In a game on January 7, 1937, Morenz was knocked down and slid into the boards. Morenz's skate jammed into the boards, and his leg snapped. Five fractures above the ankle forced him to spend weeks convalescing in hospital

On March 8, at the age of 34, he died in his sleep of a coronary embolism. More than 60 years later, Howie Morenz Jr. disclosed a nurse's long-held confession—a doctor had postponed until morning treatment for blood clots that had been detected in his leg the night of his death. A romantic legend was debunked: "When he realized that he would never play again, he couldn't live with it," Morenz's teammate Aurèle Joliat had claimed. "I think Howie died of a broken heart."

DATE OF BIRTH
Mitchell, Ontario
September 21, 1902–March 8, 1937

NHL CAREER
1923–37
Montreal, Chicago, NY Rangers

	GP	G	A	TP	PIM
RS	550	270	197	467	531
PO	47	21	11	32	68

AWARDS
1st All-Star (2), 2nd All-Star, Ross (2),
Hart (3), Stanley Cup (3), HOF 1945

Henri Richard

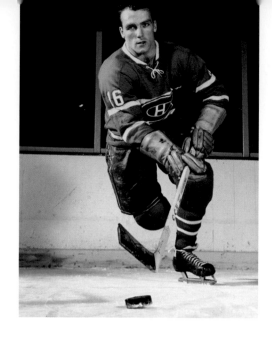

"I was just mad. I didn't really mean it," claimed Henri Richard, although he had gone on record proclaiming that Al MacNeil was the worst coach he'd ever played for. In his first term at the helm, MacNeil had benched Richard for the fifth game of the 1971 Stanley Cup finals, which had made the veteran center livid.

Richard went on to tie the deciding seventh game, then potted the winner to defeat the Chicago Blackhawks 3-2 and thereby earn his tenth Stanley Cup ring. "I could have been a bum," Richard admitted, for the Canadiens were one game away from defeat, "and instead, I was a hero." He was also gracious enough to admit that MacNeil might have successfully inspired him to greater feats, but MacNeil resigned his position anyway.

Although he was never as dynamic as his brother Maurice "The Rocket," when his little brother joined him on the Canadiens in 1955, Richard made his own mark on the game. Even after Richard's successful junior career, many thought that the Canadiens were merely placating his brother when they signed Henri, for he never grew bigger than five-foot-seven and 160 pounds. "He's a little small yet," Montreal coach Toe Blake had said in 1955, "but with his speed, we keep telling him not to try to go through the big opposition defensemen, just go around them."

"Henri Richard might have been the toughest competitor I played with."

"Once you are alone with a goaler," Richard eventually answered his critics, "size doesn't matter," but the shy, soft-spoken rookie let his first season's 19 goals do most of his talking. "Sometimes I think my size was an advantage," he noted, after heeding Blake's advice, "especially when I developed a crouching style. A big defenseman was often at a disadvantage. He'd even tumble over me if he tried to use his body rather than his stick."

Centering a line with Maurice on his right—at "The Rocket's" request—and Dickie Moore on left wing, Richard made a major contribution to the five consecutive Stanley Cup victories he enjoyed in his first five NHL campaigns. He led the league in assists in 1957–58, earning a spot on the First All-Star Team.

Moore won two scoring championships, and many felt that "The Pocket Rocket's" presence made Maurice a more complete player. From Maurice's point of view, his brother extended his career a year or two longer: Richard worked so hard, he made Maurice's job easier. In the spring of 1960, Maurice retired. Although Richard was never the goal scorer Maurice had been—

few were—he eventually set the family records for assists, points and seasons.

Blake was one of Richard's biggest boosters. "He's smart enough to be where the puck is all the time," Blake said in 1957. "He sizes up how a play is going to go, and then he gets there. And sometimes when he doesn't have things figured out in advance, he's so fast that he gets there first anyway."

Richard played doggedly, immune to intimidation—never betraying fear despite scrapping with some of the biggest and most aggressive players in the NHL. Moore expressed a sentiment shared by many: "Henri Richard might have been the toughest competitor I played with."

As goalie Gump Worsley noted, "Henri would get bounced around and always come back for more, stronger and faster than ever."

When Jean Beliveau retired in 1971, Richard assumed the team captaincy and hoisted the Stanley Cup for the last time two seasons later. Silver-haired by then, Richard continued for two more years and entered his twentieth NHL campaign. But after a broken ankle was slow to heal, he decided that he'd "better quit before it's too late." Montreal won the Cup for four consecutive years after he retired, but Richard had no regrets. His 11 Stanley Cup rings stand as a record that will never be broken.

DATE OF BIRTH
Montreal, Quebec
February 29, 1936–

NHL CAREER
1955–75
Montreal

	GP	G	A	TP	PIM
RS	1256	358	688	1046	928
PO	180	49	80	129	181

AWARDS

1st All-Star, 2nd All-Star (3), Masterton, Stanley Cup (11), HOF 1979

Milt Schmidt

The Bruins' "Kraut Line"—hard-nosed center Milt Schmidt between elegant right-winger Bobby Bauer and the tenacious Woody Dumart—was at the height of its power when World War II interrupted the trio's NHL careers. "It was our last game before we went into service," said Schmidt, recalling February 10, 1942, "and we had a fine night against the Canadiens at the Garden. I think we racked up 10 or 11 scoring points, and when the game was over, the other players on both teams picked us up on their shoulders and skated us off the ice while the crowd gave us an ovation." Although Schmidt was a member of two Stanley Cup championship teams and won the Hart Trophy in 1951, that evening in 1942 remained a personal highlight. "A man could never forget a thing like that," he fondly reminisced.

Originally known as the "Sauerkraut Line," all three Kitchener-born players shared a German heritage and an uncommon bond. "We clicked first as personalities," said Schmidt, "then as hockey players." It was Dumart and Bauer who convinced the Boston Bruins to give their young friend Schmidt a shot at an NHL career. Their loyalty was rewarded when their line became the NHL's first to finish 1-2-3 in the scoring race. Schmidt won the Art Ross Trophy, with 52 points over the 48-game 1939–40 season, and Dumart and Bauer followed with 43 points apiece.

"I never backed away from anyone. I never let up while I was on the ice."

All three returned to the NHL from the armed services, with Schmidt hitting his personal high of 62 points in the 1946–47 season, but Bauer retired at the end of that season. Schmidt and Dumart were honored together with a "Schmidt/Dumart Night" on March 18, 1952. The fans had a treat in store: Bauer suited up for the evening and scored a goal on a pass from Schmidt, and both Bauer and Dumart assisted on Schmidt's 200th NHL goal.

"[Schmidt] was tough," recalled Montreal defenseman Butch Bouchard, "a big guy, and he was one of the best skaters I ever saw. He gave me a big shift one night in my first year. When I went to the bench, Dick Irvin [Montreal's coach] asked me if I had caught a cold because of the breeze that Schmidt made when he went by me." Schmidt also served as the team "policeman" and waged a personal war with Detroit's "Black" Jack Stewart, one of the meanest defensemen in the NHL.

"Oh, we had some dandies," Schmidt laughed years later, "but we both finally wised up. We still had to earn a living!"

"I never backed away from anyone. I never let up while I was on the ice," Schmidt recalled at the end of his playing career, when he moved immediately into coaching. "I expect my players to be that way too."

"Milt will be a good coach," said Schmidt's former teammate Lynn Patrick, who stepped into the position of general manager when Schmidt replaced him as coach during the 1954–55 season, "but he'll lack one thing that has made me successful. When things get really tough for him, he won't be able to get out of the jam just by looking down the bench and yelling, 'OK, Milt, get out there.'"

It was as Boston's general manager, however, that Schmidt achieved his greatest success off the ice. In 1967, he engineered the deal that brought Phil Esposito, Ken Hodge and Fred Stanfield to Boston from Chicago, a turning point for the Bruins which led to Stanley Cup victories in 1970 and 1972.

When the Washington Capitals asked him to manage their inaugural squad in 1974, Schmidt took a brief hiatus from the Bruins organization. He fired two coaches and ensconced himself behind the bench but his team lost 95 times in 116 games. Schmidt resigned just after Christmas in 1975. Fittingly, he eventually returned to work for the Bruins, who had retired his number 15 in 1955.

DATE OF BIRTH
Kitchener, Ontario
March 5, 1918–

NHL CAREER
1936–42, 1945–55
Boston

	GP	G	A	TP	PIM
RS	778	229	346	575	466
PO	86	24	25	49	60

AWARDS

1st All-Star (3), 2nd All-Star, Ross, Hart, Stanley Cup (2), HOF 1961

Nels Stewart

Nels Stewart was known as "Old Poison," for the quick and deadly way he put the puck in the net. On January 3, 1931, he set a record that still stands, scoring two goals four seconds apart, but by then, Stewart had already established his reputation. After spending five seasons with Cleveland in the old U.S. Amateur Hockey Association, Stewart burst into the NHL with the Montreal Maroons in 1925–26. His 34 goals in the 36-game campaign led the league, as did his 42 scoring points. The Maroons won the Stanley Cup, Stewart scoring the winning goal in each of his team's victories over the Victoria Cougars in a best-of-five series.

"In some ways, 1925 was the high spot in my career, which had only started," recalled Stewart. "I won the rookie award and the Hart Trophy. I showed I could take it and dish it out too." His 119 penalty minutes were only two fewer than league leader Bert Corbeau's, and the following year, Stewart led with 133 minutes. After spending a couple of seasons on right wing, he moved to center in 1929 between ideal wingers. The "S-Line" became one of the league's most potent. "Hooley Smith and Babe Siebert did most of the work," Stewart said humbly. "They knew I was out there waiting, and if they freed the puck, I'd do the rest." Using his 200 pounds and six-foot-one frame to advantage in battling for position, Stewart also had a deft scoring touch.

"I always figured someone else could stymie the opposition; my job was to score goals."

"Goalmouth scrambles were my forte," he maintained. "I scored three-quarters of my goals by drifting in front of the goalmouth until the proper moment occurred. There's a trick in this, and I used every trick in the book." Stewart's stick had about half the average angle between shaft and blade. "I always used a lie-12, which stood almost straight up and down," he explained, "so I could control the puck close to my skates."

Back-checking was an activity that Stewart pretty much left to others. "I was a lazy daisy who hung around the goal waiting for passes," he said, but economy of movement was critical when a player was on the ice for 45 to 50 minutes of every game. "I always figured someone else could stymie the opposition," he admitted. "My job was to score goals." A slow-moving skater, he used short, choppy strides—until he got the puck.

In 1929–30, Stewart hit his career high of 39 goals and 55 points and earned a second Hart Trophy. His consistent scoring and aggressive play weren't enough to help the Maroons to a Stanley Cup victory, however, and he was traded to the Boston Bruins in 1932. He placed in the top 10 among NHL scoring leaders for three consecutive seasons before the New York Americans acquired him in 1935.

Stewart tied for the NHL lead with 23 tallies in the 1936–37 season, a noteworthy campaign that not only saw him traded back to Boston and returned to the Americans after just 10 games but also saw him pass Howie Morenz to become the league's career leader in goals scored. Stewart held that distinction for 16 years. He became the first NHL player to score 300 goals, but the end was in sight. "My reflexes were slower," he said. "I lacked that extra step, and I hit the post instead of the net."

Stewart retired after the 1938–39 season, having eclipsed Morenz's career-points record, but the Americans persuaded him to come back for one more year the next autumn. After 7 more goals, 7 assists and an almost saintly six penalty minutes in 35 games, "Old Poison" retired for good in 1940.

"Congratulations on breaking the record," read the telegram Stewart sent in 1952, the day after Maurice Richard broke his NHL career goal record of 324. "Hope it will hold for many seasons." Stewart did, however, remain the highest-scoring NHL centerman for 30 years, until another Montreal Canadien, Jean Beliveau, bettered that mark in 1964.

Stewart was a regular visitor to Maple Leaf Gardens for years. "When I see that loose puck in front of the cage," he said in 1953, "my heart still jumps. That was the moment I always waited for." Sadly, Stewart died suddenly in 1957 at the age of 55. He was elected to the Hockey Hall of Fame five years later.

DATE OF BIRTH
Montreal, Quebec
December 29, 1902–August 21, 1957

NHL CAREER
1925–40
Montreal Maroons, Boston, NY Americans

	GP	G	A	TP	PIM	AWARDS
RS	651	324	191	515	943	Ross, Hart (2), Stanley Cup,
PO	54	15	13	28	61	HOF 1962

Bryan Trottier

Over the past 25 years, Bryan Trottier has had as intimate a relationship with the Stanley Cup as any player—and then some. His six Stanley Cup rings bear testimony to his triumphs.

Trottier was selected by the Islanders in the 1974 entry draft as an underage player. He played a final year of junior hockey, and got a lucrative offer from the Cincinnati Stingers of the WHA, but Trottier had eyes only for the NHL. As he told writer Roy MacGregor during his rookie season with the Islanders, "The dream has not come true. I am *living* the dream. And that's better." Trottier tallied 98 points and won rookie-of-the-year honors and serious consideration for the Lady Byng Trophy.

While only five-foot-ten, Trottier displayed a tenacity and single-mindedness that more than compensated for his size, and as his penalty minutes grew, a nastier side emerged. "Trottier's hidden talent," said Pittsburgh coach Johnny Wilson, "is that he looks like an altar boy and hits like a monster."

When the Islanders drafted sharpshooter Mike Bossy in 1977, Trottier received the perfect winger. In 1977–78, he led the league in assists, with 77, and finished second in points behind Guy Lafleur, earning a First All-Star Team selection. Trottier followed up with an even more sensational year, adding the Art Ross and Hart trophies to his list of accomplishments. Meanwhile, his team led the league during the 1978–79 regular season and was fine-tuning its squad to challenge for the Stanley Cup.

"Trottier's hidden talent is that he looks like an altar boy and hits like a monster."

The next season, Trottier led all playoff scorers, with 12 goals and 29 points, and was awarded the Conn Smythe Trophy. The Islanders won the first of four consecutive Stanley Cups. He notched his first and only 50-goal campaign in the 1980–81 season and led the playoffs in scoring again that spring, eclipsing Bobby Orr's playoff assist record by notching 23.

But that proved to be the last time Trottier would win a scoring race. After winning their third and fourth Stanley Cups in four-game sweeps, Trottier and the Islanders slipped back into the pack during the 1983–84 regular season. They clawed their way to the Stanley Cup finals for the fifth consecutive time, but Wayne Gretzky and his Edmonton Oilers finally dethroned the Islanders.

Trottier had played for Canada in the 1981 Canada Cup tournament, but in 1984 he decided to compete for the United States—invoking his North American Indian status, which, in effect, gave him dual citizenship. "I want to give something back," he claimed, noting the United States allowed him to make a good living.

Trottier continued to rack up respectable point totals over the years, but he had also established himself as one of the game's premier checkers with his gritty play. "I'm vocal when I think my opinion will accomplish something advantageous," he said in respect to his leadership role, and he enjoyed his place in the game.

On February 13, 1990, Trottier scored his 500th career goal, but he was stunned later that spring when the Islanders bought out the last two years of his contract. The terms, unfavorable to Trottier, sent his off-ice business interests into a downward spiral. He fell into a clinical depression and financial ruin, but rebounded fully after receiving therapy and declaring bankruptcy. Pittsburgh added him to its roster, and Trottier helped the Penguins to Stanley Cup victories in 1991 and 1992.

In 1986, Trottier described how he wanted to be remembered: "As a consistently hard worker who gave his all on every shift; as a guy who, if he missed a check, kept coming back and gave that second and third effort; as a guy who just didn't quit."

DATE OF BIRTH
Val Marie, Saskatchewan
July 17, 1956–

NHL CAREER
1975–92, 1993–94
NY Islanders, Pittsburgh

	GP	**G**	**A**	**TP**	**PIM**	**AWARDS**
RS	1279	524	901	1425	912	Calder, 1st All-Star (2), 2nd All-Star (2), Ross, Hart,
PO	221	71	113	184	277	Clancy, Smythe, Stanley Cup (6) HOF 1997

Steve Yzerman

Having led the Detroit Red Wings to first-place finishes during the previous two regular seasons, Steve Yzerman had seen his team swept in the finals by New Jersey in 1995 and vanquished in the 1996 semifinals by the underdog Colorado Avalanche. That he lacked a championship ring was a knock heard against "Stevie Y" for years, but Yzerman remained undaunted. "My approach is to have fun," he said in the fall of 1996. "My desire to win the Cup hasn't changed at all, but I'm not consumed by it now.

"I want to experience the celebration of winning the Cup, of getting to carry it around the ice," he added "I've dreamed about it since I was a kid." Yzerman finally fulfilled his wish in 1997; when the Wings took their second consecutive Stanley Cup in 1998, Yzerman was awarded the Conn Smythe Trophy. In 2002, hobbled by a knee injury suffered while winning an Olympic gold medal for Canada, he completed one of the grittiest performances in playoff history by hoisting the Cup for a third time.

Yzerman made his first mark on the game through his prodigious offensive skills. His 39 goals and 87 points as an 18-year-old rookie earned him an invitation to the 1984 All-Star Game. When he was made team captain in 1986, at the tender age of 21, Yzerman blossomed with the added responsibility.

Yzerman hit the magic 50-goal season plateau in 1987–88 and topped 100 points for the first of six consecutive seasons. The following season, he peaked with 65 goals and 155 points. Only Wayne Gretzky and Mario Lemieux have ever posted higher numbers—which they did that year—but the NHL players voted "Stevie Wonder" the league's outstanding player.

"I'd like to continue to play for as long as I feel I am an effective player and getting things done on the ice."

Detroit's playoff shortcomings fueled constant speculation about whether Yzerman should be traded. "That's like asking me if I'd trade my son Jason for the kid next door," claimed Detroit's coach Jacques Demers. Although Yzerman tallied 62 goals in the 1989–90 season, the Wings missed the playoffs, and it was Demers who got the pink slip. The Yzerman trade rumors ended soon after Scotty Bowman stepped behind the bench in 1993.

Yzerman was already a strong two-way player, but Bowman insisted that he change his approach somewhat. Taking his game up another level, Yzerman sacrificed the possibility of scoring championships while still remaining an offensive threat. His inspirational shot blocking and ferocious backchecking set the tone, and within three years, his team became the league's stingiest defensively, setting an NHL record with 62 regular-season victories. A quiet man in the dressing room, Yzerman spoke volumes with his

DATE OF BIRTH
Cranbrook, British Columbia
May 9, 1965–

NHL CAREER
1983–2004
Detroit

actions, his eyes blazing with competitive fire.

Early in the 1998–99 season, he notched his 1,426th point, passing his boyhood hero Bryan Trottier and moving into tenth place on the NHL career-point list. "Bryan Trottier was my favorite player," said Yzerman, who proudly wears Trottier's old number 19. "We all have role models, and he's mine. I followed his entire career as soon as he came into the league. In some ways, I tried to play like he did. In my mind, he is one of the best players ever."

"I had set a goal of 20 years that I'd like to play," he once said. "That is not necessarily set in stone, but I'd like to continue to play for as long as I feel I am an effective player and getting things done on the ice." Major knee surgery in summer 2002 cost Yzerman most of the following season, and an eye injury knocked him out of the 2004 playoffs. Yet he still feels he has gas left in the tank. Yzerman remains the longest-serving captain of all time.

	GP	G	A	TP	PIM
RS	1453	678	1043	1721	906
PO	192	70	111	181	73

AWARDS
1st All-Star, Selke, Masterton, Pearson,
Smythe, Stanley Cup (3)

DATE OF BIRTH
Edmonton, Alberta
September 11, 1980–

NHL CAREER
2000–04
Edmonton, Philadelphia, Phoenix

Mike Comrie

As an Edmonton boy born and raised, Mike Comrie was thrilled when he pulled on his Edmonton Oilers sweater for the first time. It was the night of December 30, 2000—just hours after the signing of his first NHL contract—and the Oilers were meeting the Montreal Canadiens for a national *Hockey Night in Canada* broadcast. Comrie's dream had come true.

The son of a Canadian furniture-store magnate, Comrie was well known in Edmonton. He played two seasons for the St. Albert Saints in the Tier II Alberta Junior Hockey League; in 1997–98, he led the league in all scoring categories, with 60 goals, 78 assists and 138 points. He was voted the league's MVP and named the Canadian Junior "A" Player of the Year.

"He's strong for his size, great with the puck, has great vision and knows where everybody is at all times on the ice."

Comrie joined the University of Michigan Wolverines in 1998–99 and tallied 44 points in 42 games. But his slight build— he measured up at five-foot-nine and 172 pounds—was cause for concern. "That's the knock, and something every team has to sit down and look at. Can he overcome it?" said Edmonton Oilers director of player personnel Kevin Prendergast. "What you've got to remember with Mike is he's only an 18-year-old, playing against men. He has competitiveness. He's strong for his size, great with the puck, has great vision and knows where everybody is at all times on the ice."

The Oilers picked Comrie in the fifth round. The diminutive center returned to the Wolverines and was a finalist for the 2000 Hobey Baker Award. The Oilers beckoned, but the two sides didn't come to terms.

In 2000–01, Comrie, still eligible for junior hockey, joined the Kootenay Ice in the Western Hockey League. After 37 games he led the league in scoring with 39 goals and 79 points. Now Edmonton faced considerable pressure: If Comrie wasn't signed before the 2001 NHL draft, he would be draft eligible again. Comrie agreed to an incentive-laden, three-year contract with Edmonton worth a potential $10 million.

Comrie's first NHL goal, on January 20, 2001, was a game-winner against the powerful Detroit Red Wings. After 41 games, he had eight goals and 14 assists. Moreover, his electric style of play boded well for the future of the franchise. In July 2001, captain Doug Weight was dealt to St. Louis for purely financial reasons; Comrie's presence on the team gave some comfort to Oilers fans. He was the heir apparent.

In 2001–02, Comrie continued to surprise the opposition with his ability to thrive in physical, close-checking circumstances. At season's end, he led the Oilers with 33 goals and tied teammate Anson Carter with 60 points.

Comrie suffered a broken thumb in 2002–03, missing 13 games; on his return he played with less than his usual abandon. "He's got to play grittier," said general manager Kevin Lowe. "He's got to play an in-traffic game. The thing we've all admired most with Mike Comrie is that he's always played a fearless game, like Bobby Clarke used to play. When Mike Comrie is playing his best, he's getting his nose dirty and is in traffic." Comrie dropped to fourth in team scoring with 51 points and the Oilers bowed to Dallas in the first round of the 2003 playoffs.

That year, Comrie's contract was up for renewal and the Oilers played hardball: The young center was tendered an offer for little more than $1 million a year. He refused to sign, and Lowe locked him out of training camp. "Philosophical differences between Mike and Kevin—and they have nothing to do with money—are no less than those that would exist between Ronald Reagan and Karl Marx," said Comrie's agent, Rich Winter. "They are insurmountable."

After several acrimonious months, the Oilers traded Comrie to Philadelphia. Flyers G.M. Bobby Clarke signed Comrie to a one-year deal, and the speedy center was back living his dream in the NHL. Unfortunately, he was a poor fit on Clarke's team. Two months later, he was dealt to Phoenix. Comrie fans are certain his career will get back on track with the Coyotes.

	GP	G	A	TP	PIM
RS	241	73	84	157	177
PO	12	2	2	4	10

DATE OF BIRTH
Anchorage, Alaska
December 23, 1979–

NHL CAREER
1999–2004
New Jersey

Vincent Lecavalier

When Art Williams, the new owner of the Tampa Bay Lightning, proudly declared Vincent Lecavalier "the Michael Jordan of hockey," the ensuing disappointment was inevitable. The Lightning had just selected Lecavalier with the first pick in the 1998 NHL entry draft. Williams' hyperbole betrayed both his ignorance of the sport and the huge expectations placed upon the 18-year-old's shoulders.

Lecavalier had ripped up the Quebec Major Junior Hockey League for two seasons, culminating in 44 goals and 71 assists in a 58-game 1997–98 campaign with the Rimouski Oceanic. The six-foot-four, 205-pound center naturally drew comparisons to Mario Lemieux.

"I haven't done anything yet," Lecavalier sensibly argued. "I've only played major junior, so I don't think I should be compared to anybody. To go from major junior to the NHL is a big adjustment. This summer I'll work on my speed and strength and I'll work out with some NHL guys in August. When I get a goal in my head, I really want to reach it and my goal is to play in the NHL—if not next year then the year after that."

"He's going to be a superstar in this league for years to come."

The Lightning had no intention of returning him to junior. Although his team remained deeply mired in the NHL basement, Lecavalier posted a solid rookie season. Still, while his 13 goals and 15 assists were respectable, they were not superstar statistics. In 1999–2000, Lecavalier came more into his own, tallying 25 goals and 42 assists.

"Most definitely he's become a leader," said team captain Chris Gratton. "But the scary thing is he's working twice as hard in practice and off the ice. He's going to be a superstar in this league for years to come."

After dealing Gratton to Buffalo on March 9, 2000, the team named Lecavalier captain. Just shy of his 20th birthday, he had become the youngest full-time captain in NHL history.

In 2000–01, as Tampa Bay continued its losing ways and Lecavalier's scoring production dipped slightly, the Lightning promoted assistant coach John Tortorella. Tortorella demanded more accountability from his players, and he and Lecavalier clashed publicly several times. When contract negotiations made Lecavalier miss the start of the 2001–02 season, Tortorella stripped him of the captaincy. While the move was ostensibly to put less pressure on Lecavalier, it added fuel to the young center's belief he might be better off with another team. Before long, trade rumors were flying.

Although the team entertained offers for several months, the Lightning declared Lecavalier would remain in Tampa. After completing a 37-point campaign, it was clear Lecavalier had decided to take matters into his own hands.

"Vincent Lecavalier has demonstrated a commitment to doing everything he can from a team perspective," said Lightning general manager Jay Feaster in 2002–03, excited about his club contending for a playoff spot for the first time in seven years. "He came to camp in the best shape of his career, he spent the summer working on his faceoffs, working on his one-timers. He and John are on the same page and that, too, has been a big part of it."

"I don't blame Vinny for a lot of the things that happened last year," said Tortorella. "The things that were put on him at such an early age as a player, to me, were wrong. He's had to fight through that. When I watch him now, it's a different athlete. It's a focused athlete. He's playing in all situations. Every time he steps on the ice, he's dangerous."

Lecavalier hit career highs in 2002–03, with 33 goals and 45 helpers. More important, the Lightning went to the playoffs for only the second time.

Although teammates Brad Richards and Martin St. Louis are also major contributors to the Lightning offense, Lecavalier deserves plenty of credit for Tampa Bay's surprising 2003-04 Stanley Cup-winning season.

"We feel very confident out there," noted Lecavalier early in the campaign. "We know how to win now." He tallied 32 regular season goals and potted 9 more in the playoffs. He capped a stellar year helping Team Canada with an overtime goal en route to winning the 2004 World Cup title.

	GP	G	A	TP	PIM	AWARDS
RS	467	146	181	327	284	Stanley Cup
PO	34	12	10	22	47	

DATE OF BIRTH
Mississauga, Ontario
June 13, 1983–

NHL CAREER
2002–04
Ottawa

Jason Spezza

His arrival marked the end of Ottawa's controversial Alexei Yashin era, but Jason Spezza soon became the center of controversy himself. The Senators swapped Yashin, an almost perennial contractual problem, for the New York Islanders' Bill Muckalt, Zdeno Chara and a 2001 first-round draft pick. Ottawa promptly used the pick to select Spezza, the second player chosen overall.

Spezza had been highly touted for years, garnering national attention as early as 1998–99, when he finished his rookie junior season on the Ontario Hockey League's Brampton Battalion with 22 goals and 49 assists. He joined the Mississauga Ice Dogs for 1999–2000 and was traded to the Windsor Spitfires on November 15, 2000. Spezza tallied an impressive 36 goals and 50 assists in 41 games for Windsor, and considered his junior career over.

Spezza's skating had always been suspect, but the six-foot-two, 214-pound center had offensive talent to burn. It was his defensive play that worried Ottawa coach Jacques Martin and general manager Marshall Johnson. On the eve of the 2001–02 NHL season, Spezza was sent back to Windsor.

"I have more speed to go wide and that gives me more options."

On demoting him, Johnson referred to the NHL as "a man's league," implying that he still saw Spezza as a boy, not ready for major-league action with the Senators. A lesser team might have given him a better shot; Spezza publicly expressed his frustration at not at least starting the season with Ottawa.

Back with the Spitfires, the 19-year-old's play was uninspired. He also failed to impress at the 2001 World Junior Championships, tallying only four assists in seven games for Canada. Windsor dealt him to the Belleville Bulls in January 2002; Spezza finished his last junior season with a total of 42 goals and 63 assists.

Speculation swirled again during Ottawa's training camp for the 2002–03 campaign, and once again Spezza found himself demoted. This time he went to Binghampton of the American Hockey League, where he notched 22 goals and 32 assists in 43 games. However, the Senators called him up four times to fill in for injured players. Spezza expressed no regrets playing his 26th NHL game in April 2003, despite losing a potential

$4-million in bonuses he might have earned playing a full season as a rookie. After seeing only spot duty at times, he still managed to score 7 times and add 14 assists to his official 33-game NHL rookie year.

"I'd like to think I'll make it up [the money] through my career," laughed Spezza when reminded of the money he might have lost. "The most important thing for me is just to work hard when I get the chance."

He didn't see any playoff action until Ottawa was on the brink of elimination, but Spezza's post-season debut went wonderfully. He assisted on the winning score in the fifth game of the 2003 Eastern Conference Finals, and then potted an insurance goal. "Obviously that was a great game for me," Spezza said that night. "But playing in the last 10 games of the regular season is where I really got a lot of confidence." Ottawa took the New Jersey Devils to a seventh game before losing. The following summer, Ottawa management acknowledged that Spezza had earned a spot for the 2003–04 campaign.

"All I've had to worry about, this camp, is building chemistry with the guys," said Spezza at the Senators 2003 training camp. "I'm more confident, I'm stronger, I'm faster and I don't get bumped off the puck as much," noted Spezza. "I don't feel like I'm a step behind, ever. I know I have more speed to go wide and that gives me more options. Defensemen are going to have to respect that." He notched 22 goals and 33 assists, finishing fourth in 2003–04 team scoring. Yet coach Martin scratched him from the lineup for several playoff games. When the Sens fell to Toronto, though, Martin was sacked. Time will tell whether a new coach will make a difference, but Spezza—and Ottawa fans—are itching to see.

	GP	G	A	TP	PIM
RS	111	29	47	76	79
PO	6	1	1	2	2

DATE OF BIRTH
London, Ontario
July 2, 1979–

NHL CAREER
1997–2004
Boston

The Wingers

The Wingers

Above all else, hockey's top wingers do one thing well: put the puck into the net. Defense is not to be ignored, but without disparaging the Frank Selke Trophy—established in 1977 to reward the year's best defensive forward in the NHL—there isn't a single Selke winner here. Jari Kurri was runner-up in 1983, but he's best remembered for his dynamic goal-scoring ability.

Winning hearts and scoring titles from the flank position is a long tradition, represented in these pages by such players as Charlie Conacher in the 1930s right up to Jaromir Jagr in today's game. But all the wingers featured in *Hockey's Greatest Stars* have demonstrated strong talent and creativity in finding the net, as witnessed by their impressive personal statistics.

Toughness among these players is certainly not lacking. Maurice "The Rocket" Richard's ferocity, especially from the blue line to the net, not only earned him suspensions but general acknowledgment as hockey's greatest clutch performer. Detroit's "Terrible Ted" Lindsay lined up on left wing directly opposite Montreal's Richard for most of his career. His adage "hit 'em first" sums up the aggressive approach that helped make him a nine-time All-Star. "In this game, you have to be mean, or you're going to get pushed around," said Lindsay. "I keep telling myself to be mean. Be mean."

Lindsay's advice was taken to heart by the slightly junior "Mr. Hockey"— Gordie Howe. "If you find you can push someone around," said Howe, "then you push him around." His elbows and the damage he inflicted with them are as legendary as any other aspect of his storied career.

Yet none of the young wingers here bring a particularly nasty streak to their game. Most follow more closely in the footsteps of players such as Kurri and Johnny Bucyk, Hall of Fame scorers with a penchant for staying out of the penalty box. Hard-hitting "Big, Bad Bruin" Bucyk won the Lady Byng Trophy twice, Kurri won it once and Mike Bossy won it three times. Father-son duo Bobby and Brett Hull both collected the Byng as well, although "The Golden Jet" frequently went through, rather than around, his opponents, and the outspoken "Golden Brett" could never be described as temperate, despite his clean play.

Jagr's achievements place him solidly on the all-time-greatest list, but while his career numbers are excellent, many perceive his play in recent years as indifferent rather than inspired. Although the task is herculean, the young wingers featured here may eventually supplant Jagr or one of the retired players on the "Legends" list. It will take years of accomplishment, and the kind of rare consistency that separates the excellent players from the truly great ones. Without a doubt, the potential is there.

LEGENDS

Mike Bossy

Johnny Bucyk

Charlie Conacher

Mike Gartner

Bernie Geoffrion

Gordie Howe

Bobby Hull

Brett Hull

Jaromir Jagr

Jari Kurri

Guy Lafleur

Ted Lindsay

Frank Mahovlich

Dickie Moore

Maurice Richard

YOUNG LIONS

Marian Gaborik

Dany Heatley

Marian Hossa

Ilya Kovalchuk

Henrik Zetterberg

Opposite: Montreal Canadiens' dynamic wingers Maurice "Rocket" Richard and Dickie Moore (12) try to dig the puck out from the Toronto defense and goalie Johnny Bower. Previous page: Speedy Atlanta Thrasher Ilya Kovalchuk (17) races Toronto Maple Leaf Mats Sundin (13) for a loose puck.

Mike Bossy

A goal scorer's paradise, the Quebec junior leagues are notorious for sacrificing defense in favor of offense. Nevertheless, it was astonishing that Mike Bossy had averaged 77 goals a year over four seasons with the Laval Nationals. More surprising was that Bossy was still available in the 1977 NHL entry draft when the up-and-coming New York Islanders made their first selection.

That Bossy went 15th that year did nothing to diminish his confidence. After signing his first NHL contract, he predicted a 50-goal rookie season. Since Buffalo's Rick Martin had set the rookie scoring record six years earlier with 44 goals, Bossy's prediction sounded like a naïve boast. He admitted later that even he was surprised when he shattered the record with a 53-goal campaign. He won not only the Calder Trophy but a prestigious Second All-Star Team selection at right wing as well.

"His accuracy was uncanny at even the toughest angles."

An extraordinary goal scorer, Bossy was perhaps the greatest sniper in league history. He had an incredibly quick release with his wrist shot and could score from anywhere in the offensive zone. His accuracy was uncanny at even the toughest angles, but he was most deadly in the slot. Bossy became an integral part of the young and increasingly successful Islanders franchise, combining with center Bryan Trottier and left-winger Clark Gillies on a powerhouse line right from the beginning. Bossy followed up his rookie year with 69 goals, a career high but no fluke. His 10 NHL seasons were remarkable for his accomplishments and his consistency, and he had five seasons with 60-plus goals. Only in his last year, when the ailing back that forced his early retirement in 1987 hobbled him for most of the season, did he fail to score at least 50 goals (he still tallied 38).

Bossy set himself a lofty personal goal at the start of the 1980–81 season: He set out to score 50 goals in 50 games, an achievement matched only by the legendary Maurice "Rocket" Richard in 1944–45. Bossy started the season in fine form but needed two more goals in his 50th game, at home against the Quebec Nordiques. Quebec managed to keep him off the scoreboard until, with just over four minutes remaining, the mighty Islander power play took the ice. Bossy banged in a goal after a scramble in the crease, and the air of anticipation that had marked the night became almost electric.

Bossy got one more miraculous chance when Trottier found him unguarded and snapped a pass over with a minute and a half left in the game. Bossy rifled in goal 50. He finished the season with 68 goals and a First All-Star Team selection, his first. He then led all playoff goal scorers on his way to his second Stanley Cup. In all, he won four Cups with the Islanders, making a significant contribution with 61 playoff markers in those four consecutive years, including the final winning goals both in 1982, when he won the Conn Smythe Trophy, and in 1983.

Because of his elegant play and commitment to a nonviolent approach to the game, Bossy won the Lady Byng Trophy three times and was runner-up once. An out-spoken critic of fighting and the use of intimidation, he refused to drop his gloves even when goaded. (Of course, the presence of his linemate, Gillies, offered him a measure of protection.) Despite the machismo prevalent in the NHL, Bossy suffered little criticism for his convictions, and he always played his own style, exacting his revenge on the power play.

In attempting to dissuade Bossy from hovering anywhere near the net, many defensemen resorted to a cross-check to his back as a method of moving him away or slowing him down. Such cheap shots took their toll. After he retired, Bossy worked on a public campaign to educate minor hockey players about the danger of hitting from behind.

DATE OF BIRTH
Montreal, Quebec
January 22, 1957–

NHL CAREER
1977–87
NY Islanders

	GP	G	A	TP	PIM
RS	752	573	553	1126	210
PO	129	85	75	160	38

AWARDS

1st All-Star (5), 2nd All-Star (3), Calder, Byng (3), Smythe, Stanley Cup (4), HOF 1991

Johnny Bucyk

"It breaks your heart when a club lets your buddies go," said Johnny Bucyk late in his career, "but you can't be soft about it. It's a hard game and a hard life, and you do the best you can. It's been a good life for me." Bucyk patrolled left wing for 21 seasons in Boston, setting the club record of 545 goals that still stands. He arrived when the Bruins were serious contenders for the Stanley Cup in the 1950s; he survived the club's eight-year era of futility in the 1960s; and he was a team mainstay in the glory years of the 1970s. Even after his retirement, Bucyk has remained an active and visible Bruins employee for an additional 25 years and counting. It's difficult to picture him with any other organization, yet Bucyk played his first two NHL seasons with the Detroit Red Wings.

Bucyk grew up in Detroit's farm system, and the Red Wings thought enough of the promising winger that they gave him a Stanley Cup ring as a member of their 1955 championship team, even though he didn't actually dress for a game. He saw limited action in his rookie year the following winter, scoring only a single goal, nor did he distinguish himself greatly the next season. Meanwhile, Detroit general manager Jack Adams decided to bring goalie Terry Sawchuk—a former All-Star and Vezina Trophy winner—back from Boston.

"I never knew anyone who could hit a guy harder."

"Being traded for [Sawchuk] made me feel good," said Bucyk, "and it was the biggest break in my career. I wanted to play hockey more than anything, and knowing that I'd be getting regular ice time had me excited to get to Boston." Even better, Bucyk was reunited with former junior linemates Bronco Horvath and Vic Stasiuk, and the "Uke Line"—named for Bucyk's and Stasiuk's Ukrainian heritage—skated together for four productive seasons.

One of the heaviest forwards in the league for most of his career, Bucyk packed 220 pounds on his six-foot frame and used his bulk to advantage, banging into the corners and parking himself at the opposition net. "I never knew anyone who could hit a guy harder," noted Bobby Orr, "especially with a hip check."

Bucyk was an integral part of the "Big Bad Bruins," but he confined his aggressiveness to legal hits. "I know the Lady Byng isn't a popular trophy with the Boston fans," he said in 1970, after finishing as runner-up for the award for the second time, "but I'd sure like to win it." Bucyk's wish came true when he combined a career-high 51 goals and 65 assists with a meager eight minutes in penalties the following season. He took the Byng again in 1974 and finished just behind Marcel Dionne in 1975.

Bucyk earned his nickname "Chief" because some fans thought he looked like a native American, but others may have assumed that the title referred to his leadership position on the club. Bucyk was first named team captain in the fall of 1966, but he found his off-ice responsibilities too time-consuming and suggested that he share the load. Bucyk traded his "C" for an "A." The captainless Bruins competed for six years with as many as four alternates, but when the team won the Stanley Cup in 1970 and 1972, there was no doubt about who would raise the victory mug first.

While Bucyk hit the 50-goal plateau only once (just the fifth player at the time to do so), he was a consistent scorer. "If you're going to get goals," he explained, "you've got to get in where the action is." His hard-nosed style wasn't flashy, but he joined the 500-goal club in 1975. "I've hit more posts than nets," he said, "but the numbers are nice. I've thought of myself as a spear-carrier, not a star, really. I've just gone along getting what I could out of every game, and it's added up." Bucyk's number 9 jersey was officially retired by the Bruins when he retired in 1978.

DATE OF BIRTH
Edmonton, Alberta
May 12, 1935–

NHL CAREER
1955–78
Detroit, Boston

	GP	G	A	TP	PIM
RS	1540	556	813	1369	497
PO	124	41	62	103	42

AWARDS

1st All-Star, 2nd All-Star, Byng (2), Smythe,
Stanley Cup (2), HOF 1981

Charlie Conacher

Although some decried Toronto's Jesse Ketchum Park as a breeding ground for juvenile delinquents, hockey scouts kept a close eye on the ice rinks there. Amid a plethora of card and crap games, there was always at least one hockey game in progress, and the neighborhood hangout spawned a number of NHL players, Charlie Conacher among them. The poverty that surrounded him fueled Conacher's desire to make a career of professional hockey. "It represented money," he said. "We didn't have a pretzel. We didn't have enough money to buy toothpaste." The Maple Leafs signed Conacher into their organization in 1929, having seen his potential and bloodlines. Conacher's brother Lionel, nine years his senior, was already beginning to establish the family name as one of the greatest in Canada's sporting history.

"It felt like somebody had turned a blowtorch on me. I couldn't sit down for a week."

Lionel "Big Train" Conacher was voted Canada's Best Athlete of the Half-Century in 1950, but he was a hero in his brother's eyes long before that. Following in Lionel's footsteps, Charlie excelled at every sport he tried, particularly football, baseball, lacrosse and hockey. When Charlie saw his brother make the professional hockey ranks, he made sure his skating was top-notch. By the time Charlie had worked his way up to the Toronto Marlboros in junior hockey, Lionel had already played two NHL seasons for the Pittsburgh Pirates and was on his way to New York to play for the Americans.

When the younger Conacher graduated to the Maple Leafs in 1929, he scored 20 goals in his rookie year. One of the NHL's heftiest players, at six-foot-one and just under 200 pounds, Conacher was a sharpshooter with heavy ammunition. "It felt like somebody had turned a blowtorch on me," said Ottawa defenseman King Clancy after blocking one of Conacher's wrist shots. "I couldn't sit down for a week." Conacher led the league in goals in his second season, a feat he accomplished four more times in the next five years. Charlie "The Big Bomber" Conacher had earned his own nickname and a chance to replace Ace Bailey on Toronto's best line.

When coach Conn Smythe united Conacher with "Gentleman Joe" Primeau and Harvey "Busher" Jackson (the term busher referred to a go-getter), Toronto's original "Kid Line" was born. The combination was dynamite: Conacher scored the most goals again in the 1931–32 season; Primeau, the Lady Byng winner, had the most assists for the second consecutive year; Jackson won the scoring crown with the most points. Their line maintained a torrid pace through the playoffs, vanquishing Lionel Conacher and his Montreal Maroons in the semifinals. "The Big Bomber" continued to hit the target and led his team in goals and points—assisting on the clinching tally—to help the Leafs defeat the New York Rangers and win their first Stanley Cup in Maple Leaf Gardens in 1932.

Conacher made the Second All-Star Team a year before his defenseman brother Lionel shared that honor with him in the 1932–33 season. They both made the First Team the subsequent year. Charlie won his first scoring title, with 32 goals and 20 assists, while Lionel was steering the Chicago Blackhawks to a Stanley Cup victory. The two met head-to-head in the league finals for the first and last time in the spring of 1935, both in pursuit of their second Stanley Cup championship. Charlie had already won the scoring race again, and Lionel was back with the Montreal Maroons, who swept the Leafs in three straight games.

Conacher had one more All-Star season just ahead of him, but injuries took their toll thereafter. He played only 34 games over the next two regular seasons. The Leafs sold him to the Detroit Red Wings. Although Conacher starred for the Wings in the 1939 playoffs, he was traded that summer to the New York Americans. He put in two undistinguished years before retiring in 1941 at the age of 31.

After coaching junior hockey for several years, Conacher was hired to coach the Chicago Blackhawks in 1947. His younger brother Roy was his best player and won the Art Ross Trophy as scoring champion in 1949. Conacher retired again a year before his son Pete, the next member of hockey's "royal family," made it to the NHL in 1951.

DATE OF BIRTH
Toronto, Ontario
December 20, 1909–December 30, 1967

NHL CAREER
1929–41
Toronto, Detroit, NY Americans

	GP	G	A	TP	PIM	AWARDS
RS	460	225	173	398	523	1st All-Star (3), 2nd All-Star (2),
PO	49	17	18	35	53	Ross (2), Stanley Cup, HOF 1961

Mike Gartner

Filling in for injured teammate Mark Messier at the 1993 All-Star Game, Mike Gartner not only won the skating race in the NHL Skills Competition but took away a car as the prize for being named the game's most valuable player. Opening the scoring with two goals only 22 seconds apart on his way to a first-period hat trick, Gartner contributed a fourth goal in the second period, helping the Wales Conference set an All-Star Game scoring record in a 16-6 blowout. "I'll give Mark a big handshake," he laughed when asked whether he owed Messier anything, "but not the car!"

"My speed was a God-given thing."

Gartner was the quietest member of a select group. On December 15, 1997, he became only the fifth NHL player to register 700 goals in a career. Like Gordie Howe, another "700 Club" member, Gartner never erupted for a 60- or 70-goal season, but he did hit the prestigious 50-goal mark in the last game of the 1984–85 season. The key to Gartner's success was consistency. He holds the NHL record with 17 seasons of 30 or more goals, with 15 of those seasons in succession. The lockout-shortened 1994–95 season interrupted his unprecedented streak, but trades never broke his stride. Gartner is the only player who has scored 30 or more goals for five different teams.

In 1978, Gartner made a bold move when he signed as an underage free agent with the WHA's Cincinnati Stingers. When the NHL swallowed the rival league the next year, the Washington Capitals made Gartner the league's number-four draft pick. Generous amounts of ice time on a weak Washington team translated into more goals than even Gartner knew he was capable of scoring. Although convinced that his strength lay in his two-way play, Gartner found his niche as a fleet sniper. "My speed was a God-given thing," said Gartner. "I worked on it, but for the most part, it was there from the very beginning, when I was a kid." He established franchise records for career goals and points (since bettered by Peter Bondra), but after 10 years with the Capitals, Gartner was traded for the first time in March 1989 to the Minnesota North Stars.

Although Gartner tallied more than a point a game for Minnesota, he was sent to the New York Rangers a year later. He had three consecutive 40-goal years in Manhattan. The 1991–92 season was an especially auspicious one: He recorded his 500th goal, 500th assist and 1,000th point and played in his 1,000th NHL game. All cylinders were firing as the Rangers headed toward their first Stanley Cup victory in over 40 years. But at the 1994 trading deadline, Gartner was dealt to the Toronto Maple Leafs. Gartner himself never played on a Stanley Cup winner.

Gartner completed two solid seasons for the Leafs before he was sent to Phoenix. The 36-year-old proved that he still had wings when he won the NHL skating race for the third time at the 1996 All-Star Game. "You knew if you got him the puck, he could make things happen," said Larry Murphy, who played with Gartner in Washington, Minnesota and Toronto. "When you played against him, you had to respect his speed. You had to back off him or he'd burn you." But Gartner battled injuries in 1997–98, for the first time in his career, and Phoenix didn't renew his contract.

Gartner had free-agent status but he honored a commitment he had made to his wife and children—to be settled at that point in their lives. "Maybe I'm leaving something on the table," he said in announcing his retirement, "but 20 years from now, will it matter if I scored 780 goals instead of 708? Will it matter if I played 22 years instead of 19?" Gartner bowed out gracefully and took up a full-time position with the NHL Players' Association.

DATE OF BIRTH
Ottawa, Ontario
October 29, 1959–

NHL CAREER
1979–98
Washington, Minnesota, NY Rangers, Toronto, Phoenix

	GP	G	A	TP	PIM	AWARDS
RS	1432	708	627	1335	1159	HOF 2001
PO	122	43	50	93	125	

Bernie Geoffrion

Bernie Geoffrion invented the slap shot in his youth, and when he brought it to the big leagues, it was unlike anything the NHL had ever seen. "It's definitely harder than anything [Charlie] Conacher shot," claimed Toronto coach Hap Day, who played with Conacher in the 1930s. "I watched Geoffrion closely on one play. I saw him draw the stick back, but I didn't see the puck until it bounced off the goalpost."

Geoffrion's nickname "Boom-Boom" referred to the sound of the puck reverberating off the end boards, but he hit twine often enough that the Montreal Canadiens were clamoring for his services while he was still a teenager. He had joined Montreal's junior team at the age of 14 and more than held his own, and he continued to improve his entire game while paying particular attention to the shot that would make him famous. Geoffrion held out until there were only 18 games left in the Canadiens' 1950–51 season, potting eight goals but still preserving his rookie status for the following year. He then won the coveted Calder Trophy, with 30 goals and 24 assists.

"I didn't see the puck until it bounced off the goal post."

Geoffrion had a glorious career with the Canadiens; his name went on the Stanley Cup six times. He scored more than 20 goals per season a dozen times for Montreal—when that total really meant something in the NHL. Unfortunately, Maurice Richard (who also patrolled right wing for Montreal), Detroit's Gordie Howe and Andy Bathgate of the Rangers were such outstanding players that it was difficult for Geoffrion to gain league-wide recognition of his considerable talents. Even after Geoffrion won the scoring championship in the 1954–55 season, Richard was named to the First All-Star Team. Geoffrion's resulting anger, however, was nothing compared with that of the fans in the Montreal Forum when Richard was suspended for the last few games of the season and Geoffrion passed him to earn the scoring title by a single point.

"I couldn't deliberately *not* score," complained Geoffrion, but the boos and catcalls rained down on him regardless. "I was sick of the whole thing," an emotional Geoffrion later confessed. "Even thinking about hockey made me throw up. I wanted to get away from hockey. But [Jean] Beliveau and [Maurice] Richard visited me. They urged me to stay in the game."

Even after Richard retired in 1960 and Geoffrion won his second Art Ross Trophy in 1960–61, with only the second 50-goal campaign in NHL history, some fans continued to harbor resentment that "Boom-Boom" had again entered Richard's territory. But it all ended happily: Most of the Forum gave Geoffrion a standing ovation, he made the First All-Star Team, and he added the Hart Trophy as the league's MVP.

Geoffrion called it quits after the 1963–64 season. He then coached for two years for the Canadiens' organization in the minor leagues. When the step up the ladder that he believed had been promised him didn't materialize, he severed his long relationship with Montreal.

Geoffrion arrived in New York in 1966, although not as coach. He made a remarkable comeback and reentered the NHL ranks as a player with the Rangers. He helped the team into the playoffs twice—he never missed the playoffs over 16 seasons in total—before deciding to retire for good in 1968.

He briefly coached the Rangers, then the Atlanta Flames for their first few seasons in the early 1970s and made a celebrated but short-lived return to Montreal in 1979. But his nerves and personality weren't suited for coaching. He returned to Atlanta and eventually helped his adopted hometown regain an NHL franchise.

DATE OF BIRTH
Montreal, Quebec
February 14, 1931–

NHL CAREER
1951–64, 1966–68
Montreal, New York Rangers

	GP	G	A	TP	PIM
RS	883	393	429	822	689
PO	132	58	60	118	88

AWARDS

1st All-Star, 2nd All-Star (2), Calder, Ross (2), Hart, Stanley Cup (6), HOF 1972

Gordie Howe

Affectionately known as "Mr. Hockey," Gordie Howe is the most durable and consistent star ever to lace on skates. Not only did he play 26 NHL seasons, but he dominated the league for most of that time. In his 23rd NHL season, he reached his highest point total of 103. For 20 consecutive years, he finished among the top five scorers in the league, and he garnered 21 All-Star Team selections. In today's game, he would be regarded as a "power forward," but his teammates simply called him "The Power."

On the ice, Howe deferred to no one. Detroit general manager Jack Adams had to pull him aside after his first three NHL seasons and point out that he needn't have a punch-out with every player in the league. Howe curbed his fighting, which seemed to translate directly into more goals, but he remained one of the nastiest players in the game. He was just more subtle about it.

His teammates simply called him "The Power."

Howe had a rare ambidextrous shooting ability, but he also possessed the "sharpest" elbows in the league. "We had very poor equipment and I have very sloping shoulders," he has explained. "It was almost a necessity to get my elbow out." But Howe wasn't opposed to wielding his stick as a weapon either, and he used his awesome strength in surprising ways. "When a guy was a little faster than me and we were going behind the net," he once laughed, "I'd swing a little wide to give him the inside spot, then squeeze him off so he'd run into the net. A lot of guys have told me, 'Oh, I knew when I was halfway through there, I was in trouble.'"

While Howe notched only seven goals as a rookie, he impressed the Red Wings enough to be placed on a line with slick Sid Abel and feisty sniper Ted Lindsay in his second season. Before long, the "Production Line" was tearing up the league. After losing the Stanley Cup finals two years in succession, Howe tried to ram Toronto's Ted Kennedy into the boards in the first game of the 1950 playoffs. Kennedy ducked, and Howe crashed into the boards headfirst. Rushed to hospital, for a while it looked as if he might not live through the night. In time, Howe made a full recovery.

The early 1950s were Detroit's glory years (four Stanley Cups in six seasons), and although the Cup eluded him thereafter, Howe maintained his personal excellence through thick and thin. Still racking up points but suffering constant pain with arthritis, he retired in 1971. At the age of 43, Howe moved into a front-office "executive" position. He hated it, desperately wanting to be more than a ribbon cutter. So in 1973, when the newly formed WHA invited him to join his young sons Mark and Marty on a line for the Houston Aeros, he jumped at the chance. Howe was an All-Star again and added 174 goals and 334 assists to his career totals. Howe regarded the six seasons spent playing with his boys in the WHA the highlight of his 33 years in professional hockey.

Despite hints of disappointment at having his NHL career goal-scoring record broken by Wayne Gretzky, Howe has always maintained an amiable relationship with Gretzky, who has idolized Howe since he was a boy. The last time their paths crossed in a meaningful way on the ice was in 1980, when Gretzky played in his first NHL All-Star Game and Howe played his last. The loyalties of the 21,000 fans in Detroit's Joe Louis Arena were loud and clear. "I didn't know what to do with myself," Howe admitted later, for it seemed the standing ovation for him would never end. "It's still hard to accept appreciation. I'd love to show that I accept this with a great amount of gratitude, but how do you do it?" A few months later, at age 52, Howe hung up his skates for good.

DATE OF BIRTH
Floral, Saskatchewan
March 31, 1928–

NHL CAREER
1946–71, 1979–80
Detroit, Hartford

	GP	G	A	TP	PIM	AWARDS
RS	1767	801	1049	1850	1685	1st All-Star (12), 2nd All-Star (9), Ross (6),
PO	157	68	92	160	220	Hart (6), Stanley Cup (4), HOF 1972

Bobby Hull

"The Golden Jet" electrified NHL audiences for 15 seasons with his tremendous speed, muscular good looks and unprecedented goal-scoring ability. "You knew what he was going to do—you could read him like a book," maintained Gordie Howe, "but he was so strong, he'd do it anyway."

And yet all that power was tempered by good grace. "Always keep your composure," advised Bobby Hull, who won the Lady Byng Trophy in 1965. "You can't score from the penalty box; and to win, you have to score." While Hull owns only one Stanley Cup ring, the goals and the wins certainly came for him. In 1965–66, he became the last NHL scoring champion to win with more goals than assists, and for seven seasons, he led the league in goals scored.

An outspoken critic of violence in hockey, Hull even staged a one-man one-game strike during the 1977–78 season to publicize his cause. Yet he systematically terrorized opposition goalies, cranking noisy shots off the glass during warm-ups and publicly discussing his strategy of firing his first shots in a game at the goalie's head. Netminder Gump Worsley challenged Hull bare-faced over 15 seasons, maintaining that Hull only talked of firing the hard high one and, instead, rifled in a low shot, but most goalies were instinctively back on their heels.

"He needs another shot like I need a hole in the head, which I may get."

When his teammate Stan Mikita started experimenting with a curved stick in the early 1960s, Hull joined him in tinkering with the new weapon. The "banana blade" was born, and Hull was thrilled with the results. "If you don't quite catch all of the puck as you let it go, it'll rise or drop suddenly, depending on the spin," he explained in 1966. "Drawing it toward you as you let it go sets up a different spin that produces a curve."

With 54 goals in the 1965–66 season, Hull broke the long-standing record of 50 goals in a season (he'd previously matched the records of Maurice Richard and Bernie Geoffrion); the following season, he tallied 52 goals. Toronto netminder Johnny Bower complained, "He needs another shot like I need a hole in the head, which I may get."

In 1967, the NHL stepped in with a new rule limiting a stick's curve, and when Hull broke his own record in 1968–69 with 58 goals, the league further limited the curve. Yet it would be a gross overstatement to claim that the hooked blade was the key to Hull's success. Many experts believe that he would have scored more than 70 goals in 1968–69 without the big curve, suggesting that it impeded his accuracy.

Hull's career scoring record is impressive. He won the Art Ross Trophy three times, and of the 10 first 50-goal seasons, five were his. Although he left the Chicago Blackhawks while still in his prime, he holds most of that franchise's career goal-scoring records.

Hull rocked the hockey world when he signed with the Winnipeg Jets of the upstart WHA in 1972. All the new franchises ponied up to give Hull a million-dollar signing bonus on top of the Jets' record-breaking salary offer, and Hull (who had initially made an outrageous demand just to get the WHA to leave him alone) felt compelled to accept the lucrative deal. "If I told you the big contract had nothing to do with my signing," he admitted after, "I'd be lying," but he cited a long-standing complaint about how Chicago had negotiated with him over the years. Almost immediately, every professional hockey player was able to command more money, for if a living legend such as Hull could jump to the new league, who couldn't?

Hull added 303 goals and 335 assists in just over six WHA seasons, most as left wing on a line with the elegant Swedes Anders Hedberg and Ulf Nilsson. He retired from hockey in the fall of 1978, but when the Jets joined the NHL the following year, he made a brief comeback. Hobbled by injuries and after a nine-game stint with the Hartford Whalers, he retired again before the season was out. Hull's number 9 jersey was eventually raised to the rafters in both Winnipeg and Chicago.

DATE OF BIRTH
Pointe Anne, Ontario
January 3, 1939–

NHL CAREER
1957–72, 1979–80
Chicago, Winnipeg, Hartford

	GP	G	A	TP	PIM	AWARDS
RS	1063	610	560	1170	640	1st All-Star (10), 2nd All-Star (2), Ross (3),
PO	119	62	67	129	102	Hart (2), Byng, Stanley Cup, HOF 1983

Brett Hull

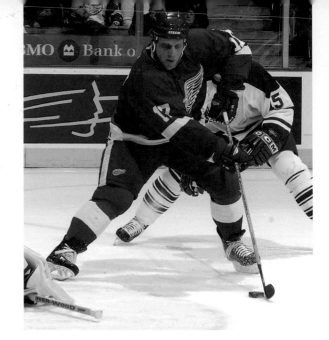

"I'm a goal scorer," says Brett Hull. "That's not all I do, but that's what I do best." Hockey scouts were always convinced about Hull's sniping skills but not about whether he could play at the NHL level. As the son of Hall of Fame legend Bobby Hull, "The Golden Jet," Brett naturally attracted attention when he tallied 105 goals as a Junior B player to close out his teenage years. But at the same age, his father had been rifling in goals for the Chicago Blackhawks.

"Maybe I've got his genes, but I definitely don't have his personality," says Brett. "You're talking to the laziest man alive. I'm not into expending physical energy. I'm into expending mental energy. On the ice, my dad was like a thoroughbred. I'm more like a train. I chug."

The Calgary Flames decided to risk their sixth draft pick and made Hull the 117th player chosen in 1984. He also earned an invitation to the University of Minnesota at Duluth, where he potted 84 goals in 90 games over two seasons. A year with Moncton in the AHL followed, and on the strength of 50 goals and 42 assists, he got the long-awaited call-up to the Flames in the spring of 1987.

"My dad was like a thoroughbred. I'm more like a train. I chug."

Doubts about his work ethic persisted, even through his official rookie year of 1987–88, when he tallied 26 goals and 50 points in 52 games. The Flames made a trade—debatable even then—dealing Hull to the St. Louis Blues in 1988. The move soon looked downright foolish.

Hull maintained his solid scoring pace with the Blues, contributing 7 playoff goals in 10 games and leading his new club with 41 goals and 43 assists in the 1988–89 season. Magic ensued the following year, though. Newly acquired centerman Adam Oates, one of hockey's slickest passers, helped "The Golden Brett" score 72 goals, a record for right-wingers. Hull shattered his own mark with 86 goals in the 1990–91 season and added 70 more the year after. Only Wayne Gretzky has ever found the net more often over a three-season span.

In addition to making the First All-Star Team three times running, Hull added the Lady Byng Trophy in 1990, and both the Hart and Lester Pearson trophies in 1991. "My whole game is based on deception," he explained. "I'm there, and then I'm not. I don't want to be noticed. I barely raise my arms when I score. I don't want people mad at me for making them look stupid."

Hull's production slackened over the next half-dozen seasons with the Blues, yet he still scored an average of more than 40 goals a year. He endured a lengthy feud with coach Mike Keenan, who ultimately lost the public battle and was sacked. Hull has always been unafraid of controversy. He angered league officials by complaining about the interference that he and other finesse players faced nightly. "It's not the referees' fault," said Hull. "It's the people above them. They're ruining the game. It's embarrassing. I wouldn't pay money to watch that. The game's going to hell in a handbasket."

Hull signed a free-agent contract with Dallas in July 1998, and hit two milestones with the Stars. "It's a weird feeling," he said. "You hope to get one goal in this game, but to say I have 500 goals and 1,000 points is a thrill. I'll long remember this night." Hull capped a memorable season by scoring the 1999 Stanley Cup-winning goal in overtime.

After three seasons in Dallas, Hull joined the Detroit Red Wings for 2001–02, and supped again from the Cup at the end of the season. He surpassed his father's 610 career NHL goals in 2000, and notched his 700th goal in February 2003. On the move again, he has struck a deal with the Pheonix Coyotes.

DATE OF BIRTH
Belleville, Ontario
August 9, 1964–

NHL CAREER
1986–2004
Calgary, St Louis, Dallas, Detroit, Phoenix

	GP	G	A	TP	PIM
RS	1264	741	649	1390	458
PO	202	103	87	190	73

AWARDS

1st All-Star (3), Hart, Byng, Pearson,
Stanley Cup (2)

Jaromir Jagr

The wild mane of curly hair no longer spills onto his shoulders from beneath his helmet, but Jaromir Jagr may be best remembered as the rebellious youth who roared onto the NHL scene in 1990. He was a spectacular sight, tearing down the ice with the puck seemingly tied to his stick with a string. His boyish good looks added to his charm, yet his juvenile attitude diminished his accomplishments at times. His military salute after scoring—a tribute, he maintained, to his grandfather—was seen by most opponents as a cocky taunt. Jagr wore sweater number 68 in memory of the same grandfather, who died in a Czechoslovakian jail as a political prisoner in 1968.

Born in 1972, four years after Soviet Union tanks rolled in to strengthen a threatened Communist government, Jagr came of age during the next Czechoslovak uprising. Fortunately, the "Velvet Revolution" wasn't quashed, and Jagr became the first hockey player from his country to attend an NHL draft without having to defect. The Pittsburgh Penguins picked him early in the first round of the 1990 NHL entry draft.

Someone soon discovered that "Jaromir" was an anagram for "Mario Jr.," and indeed, Jagr seemed cut from the same cloth as team captain Lemieux. At six-foot-two and 230 pounds, he has Lemieux's reach, strength and stickhandling ability. His 27 goals and 30 assists in his rookie year helped the Penguins into first place in their division, and he added 13 playoff points toward Pittsburgh's first Stanley Cup victory in 1991. The following year, he was a dominant factor in defending the Cup, scoring 11 goals and 13 assists in the playoffs.

"There's so much innocence to him," said veteran Gordie Roberts in 1992. "He enjoys everything. He hasn't realized yet that hockey is a business."

During Lemieux's season off to convalesce from Hodgkin's disease, Jagr edged out Eric Lindros to take the 1994–95 scoring title. Lemieux returned the following year and Jagr erupted with his most productive season, scoring 62 goals and 87 assists. He finished second to Lemieux in the race for the Art Ross Trophy.

"You always want to score a beautiful goal," says Jagr. "That's what you're trying to do. Score some goals like that, get more confidence for the other ones." Yet his scoring crown in 1997–98 came on the strength of his league-leading 67 assists. One of the most artistic and creative players of all time, Jagr also barges to the net, drawing hooks, slashes and power-play opportunities.

"Playing with him is a lot of fun," said Stu Barnes in 1998. "You never know what you're going to see next. But he's also a guy who really works hard off the ice, and that's something he doesn't get enough credit for." With Mario Lemiux in retirement, Jagr was given the team captaincy in the summer of 1998, when Ron Francis left the team through free agency.

He was scoring champ again in 1998–99 and 1999–2000 and won a fifth Art Ross Trophy with a 52-goal, 69-assist campaign the following season. Unfortunately for Pittsburgh fans, the franchise's financial woes prompted trades of most of the team's high-priced talent. Jagr was dealt to the Washington Capitals, who signed him to a long-term, $11-million per season contract in the summer of 2001.

He led the Capitals in 2001–02 with 79 points in 69 games and with 77 points in 2002–03. But Washington too went on a cost-cutting spree, and the Caps dealt Jagr to the NY Rangers in the middle of the 2003-04 season.

Not long ago, Jagr was advising his line-mates in Pittsburgh: "I don't want us chasing the puck down; that's how you get tired. Just keep it on my stick." Rangers fans wish he consistently exhibited that same hunger for the puck today. When Jagr is "on his game," it couldn't be in better hands.

DATE OF BIRTH
Kladno, Czechoslovakia
February 15, 1972–

NHL CAREER
1990–2004
Pittsburgh, Washington, NY Rangers

	GP	G	A	TP	PIM
RS	1027	537	772	1309	699
PO	146	67	87	154	123

AWARDS
1st All-Star (4), 2nd All-Star, Ross (3),
Hart, Pearson, Stanley Cup (2)

Jari Kurri

"There was a tremendous load off the back of the entire team," admitted Jari Kurri after the Edmonton Oilers won the Stanley Cup in 1990, "because we demonstrated that we weren't a one-man show." Kurri, who earned his fifth Stanley Cup ring with that win, probably felt more relief than anyone else on the Oilers team. When Wayne Gretzky had been traded to the Los Angeles Kings in 1988, many said that Kurri would be ordinary without him. The two had been the dominant offensive pairing of the 1980s, but Kurri proved his critics wrong. In his first NHL season without Gretzky, Kurri made the Second All-Star Team with a 44-goal 58-assist campaign. During the 1990 Stanley Cup playoffs, he scored 10 goals and added 15 assists.

While Gretzky was at the peak of his offensive power in Edmonton, Kurri made more of a contribution than was sometimes acknowledged. Gretzky himself is always the first to credit his teammates for his success, and no one was closer to Gretzky than Kurri. In the end, the two played 13 seasons together. "We see the game the same way," said Gretzky. Coming from "The Great One," this is a generous compliment. The two seemed to operate on an intuitive level: Kurri found his way to open ice, Gretzky found him with the puck, and Kurri had the "soft" hands to finish the play. He also made great passes; his 797 career assists are proof that he was a premier playmaker too.

"I back-check all those years for you, and that's how you treat me?"

Kurri was also more than an offensive force. He was runner-up to Bobby Clarke in voting for the 1983 Frank Selke Trophy, but it's surprising that Kurri never won that award as the league's best defensive forward. Perhaps his offensive numbers threw the voters off. Assigned to Gretzky's line after a number of players had auditioned, Kurri knew from the start that two-way play would be critical to his success. He earned league-wide respect for his clean defensive play (he was also a Lady Byng Trophy winner) but still had six 100-point seasons. Kurri had a career year in 1984–85, setting a new high for right-wingers with 71 goals and finishing with 135 points. He led the league with 68 tallies the following season.

Still, Kurri somehow managed to save his best hockey for the playoffs. He was the leading playoff goal scorer four times—the Oilers won the Cup on each occasion—and he shares a record with Philadelphia's Reggie Leach for 19 playoff goals in one season. Kurri's two overtime markers, seven hat tricks and 10 shorthanded scores lifted him to third place on both the all-time playoff goals and points lists at the end of his career.

A contract dispute in 1990–91 led to a year of play in Italy before a three-team trade sent Kurri to the Los Angeles Kings. Reunited with Gretzky for two seasons, he helped the Kings to the 1993 Stanley Cup finals. He was traded to the New York Rangers in 1996.

Kurri's defensive game had become his primary contribution, and he bounced to several teams before finishing his career in 1997–98 with the Colorado Avalanche. Shortly after notching his 600th career goal, he played for the World Team (players born outside North America) at the 1998 All-Star Game. Kurri scored a goal but Gretzky slipped a pass by him to Mark Messier, who scored the game-winner for the North American side. "Wayne still fools even me," laughed Kurri. "I told him at the face-off: 'I back-check all those years for you, and that's how you treat me?'"

In 2001, Kurri became the first Finnish player to enter the Hockey Hall of Fame. The Edmonton Oilers retired his number 17 sweater the same year.

DATE OF BIRTH
Helsinki, Finland
May 18, 1960–

NHL CAREER
1980–90, 1991–98
Edmonton, Los Angeles, NY Rangers, Anaheim, Colorado

	GP	G	A	TP	PIM
RS	1251	601	797	1398	545
PO	200	106	127	233	123

AWARDS

1st All-Star (2), 2nd All-Star (3), Byng, Stanley Cup (5), HOF 2001

Guy Lafleur

When he got the puck on his stick, the Montreal Forum crowd came alive with cries of "Guy! Guy!" The fans edged forward in their seats, anticipating at least an exciting play if not a goal. And the focus of their attention, Guy Lafleur, rarely disappointed.

Heralded as a franchise player when he was drafted by the Montreal Canadiens in 1971, Lafleur began his career with a heavy responsibility. Many saw him as a replacement for the legendary Jean Beliveau, who had retired the same year. Lafleur had created high expectations with an extraordinary junior career, tallying 130 goals and 79 assists in his last season with the Quebec Remparts.

While Lafleur's rookie NHL campaign was excellent by normal standards (29 goals and 35 assists), he followed up with seasons of 55 and 56 points and was frequently portrayed by the media as a disappointment. In truth, Montreal boasted an incredible lineup and intentionally broke in rookies slowly.

Lafleur's attempt at a comeback caught most fans totally off guard.

Lafleur finally had a breakthrough year in the 1974–75 season, with 53 goals and 66 assists, and many cited as a factor his decision to shed the headgear he had worn for his first three years in Montreal. Whether or not having the wind blow through his hair made Lafleur feel more creative and reckless, as some claimed, it certainly wouldn't have been quite the same for the fans if he'd had a helmet on. As he danced and whirled up the ice, "The Flower" was a beautiful sight, and Lafleur became a huge box-office draw as the first player to have six consecutive 50-goal and 100-point seasons.

Induction into the Hockey Hall of Fame represents the pinnacle of a successful hockey career. A player basks in the spotlight, while he and others reflect on his accomplishments and past glories. Not so for Lafleur. In 1988, while others were fondly looking back at his three scoring championships and five Stanley Cup victories with the Montreal Canadiens, Lafleur was anxiously looking ahead. He was only days away from finding out whether he could skate his way back into the NHL after three years of an unsatisfactory retirement.

Lafleur's attempt at a comeback caught most fans totally off guard. But Lafleur's retirement in 1985 had not been freely chosen. Although in 1978, Lafleur had described hockey as "like a dream to me," by 1984, it had become a nightmare. Former teammate and then coach Jacques Lemaire imposed a tightly controlled defensive system that stifled Lafleur's natural gifts. Since Lafleur's game was offense, he saw a decreasing amount of ice time, poison to any scorer. Soon, some of the fans were starting to get on his back, for even when he got on the ice, Lafleur showed little of his famous flash and creativity. Handcuffed by Lafleur's stature, team management ignored his appeals for a trade, so Lafleur quit in frustration. For three years, he missed the game terribly.

When the New York Rangers beckoned with the offer of a tryout in 1988, Lafleur proved that he could still play in the NHL. He had a decent season, with 18 goals and 27 assists, and played two more seasons after that with the Quebec Nordiques. Age was finally catching up with him and his performance was only average, but Lafleur had succeeded in proving to himself and to everyone else that he could have been a contributing player during his forced "sabbatical."

When Lafleur finally announced his forthcoming retirement in 1991, on his terms, he received an appreciative acknowledgment from every crowd in every city, but especially in Montreal. All past indignities and disputes were buried, and Lafleur later happily took an off-ice job as one of the Montreal Canadiens' exalted ambassadors.

DATE OF BIRTH
Thurso, Quebec
September 20, 1951–

NHL CAREER
1971–85, 1988–91
Montreal, NY Rangers, Quebec

	GP	G	A	TP	PIM	AWARDS
RS	1126	560	793	1353	399	1st All-Star (6), Ross (3), Hart (2), Pearson (3),
PO	128	58	76	134	67	Smythe, Stanley Cup (5), HOF 1988

Ted Lindsay

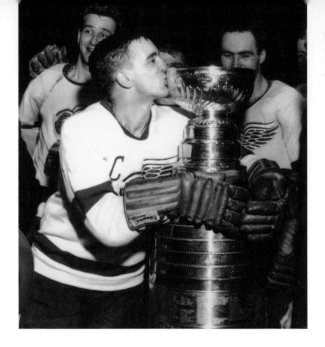

Detroit hockey fans can thank Lady Luck for making Ted Lindsay a Red Wing. After Lindsay played well in his first game for Toronto's St. Mike's junior team, the Maple Leafs brass was alerted that the school had a rookie forward the Leafs should consider. At a subsequent game, the Toronto scouts put the best forward they saw on the ice on their "protected" list, making him their property. Unknown to them, however, this forward was not Lindsay—he had been knocked out of the lineup with a severe gash in his leg.

When the still-hobbled Lindsay resumed playing, he attracted little notice. By January, he was fully healed and showing the feisty vigor for which he would become legendary. In 1944, the day after a game against Detroit's junior affiliate, Lindsay was signed by the Red Wings organization.

"Terrible" Ted Lindsay was short of stature and temper. He eventually retired as the most penalized player of all time. Lindsay played a mean game, and the damage he inflicted often led to bloody retaliation, as indicated by the 700 stitches he took in his face during his career. But the league's most hated player earned nothing but appreciation in Detroit.

"He's the guy who holds us together," claimed Sid Abel, the center of the famous "Production Line" between Lindsay and Gordie Howe. "He keeps us at a high pitch. He won't allow anyone to let down when he's on the ice."

"As long as the fans don't boo you at home, you don't have to worry."

Lindsay commanded respect off the ice as well. "It was all in the tone of his voice," said Howe. "It was very authoritative."

And Lindsay wasn't hesitant about taking the initiative. He captained the Red Wings to a Stanley Cup victory in 1954. After the final game, the Stanley Cup was placed on a table at center ice, and the winning team stood around it drinking champagne. But Lindsay had a different idea. "It was an impulsive sort of thing," he later explained. He hoisted the Cup over his head and skated a lap around the ice near the boards to give the jubilant fans a better look. A tradition was born.

"As long as the fans don't boo you at home, you don't have to worry," he said in 1957. "If they boo you on the road, you must be doing something to help your own club. As for the other players, I'd like them all to be my friends—off the ice." The latter admission reflected a new approach, for in previous years, Lindsay admittedly "hated" his opposition *all* the time. But the injustices he saw inflicted, especially on less successful players, inspired him to form a Players' Association in 1956. Secret meetings were held until January 1957, when the first Players' Association press conference stunned league owners. Their rage was eventually vented on all the key figures.

Despite the distraction of his off-ice activity, Lindsay enjoyed his most productive NHL season in 1956–57, tallying 30 goals and 55 assists. But the following summer, he was dealt to the cellar-dwelling Chicago Blackhawks—as close to exile as existed in the NHL then—along with the outspoken young goalie Glenn Hall. Toronto's Conn Smythe sent his troublemakers to Chicago as well, and the threat of further retaliation against the Players' Association killed Lindsay's organization effort.

In the spring of 1960, Lindsay retired from hockey and returned to Detroit. He made a brief but successful one-season comeback in 1964–65, after Sid Abel became Detroit's general manager. "Emotionally," said Lindsay, "I'd never left."

DATE OF BIRTH
July 29, 1925–
Renfrew, Ontario

NHL CAREER
1944-60, 1964-65
Detroit, Chicago

	GP	G	A	TP	PIM
RS	1068	379	472	851	1808
PO	133	47	49	96	194

AWARDS
1st All-Star (8), 2nd All-Star, Ross,
Stanley Cup (4), HOF 1966

Frank Mahovlich

Few superstars have been unappreciated for as long as Frank Mahovlich, who spent nearly 11 years in a love-hate relationship with the Toronto Maple Leafs. Mahovlich burst onto the NHL scene in the 1957–58 season, edging out Bobby Hull in Calder Trophy voting for rookie of the year. The Leafs managed to get to the Stanley Cup finals the following two seasons, but the team's new savior couldn't quite take them to the promised land. That all looked to change when Mahovlich erupted with 38 goals in the first 35 games of the 1960–61 season. He eventually set the club record with 48 goals at season's end, but he was seen by some as a disappointment. A pattern had been set.

"No one else is so elegant, so electric, so furious, so fluid," wrote Peter Gzowski in 1961. "Other skaters stride, he swoops. They glide, he soars. They sprint, he explodes." But Toronto's coach and general manager Punch Imlach wanted his team to dominate through defense and rigid positional play. While Mahovlich scored dozens of beautiful goals in helping the Leafs win three consecutive Stanley Cups in 1962, 1963 and 1964, the autocratic Imlach encouraged Mahovlich—and the fans and media—to believe that there should have been dozens more goals.

"It was as if a piano had been lifted off my back."

"If Toronto fans would appreciate his great talent and give him the cheers he deserves instead of booing him," said Gordie Howe in the mid-1960s, "maybe the pressure wouldn't cook the guy." The soft-spoken Mahovlich suffered two nervous breakdowns and was sent to hospital both times with a diagnosis of deep depression and tension.

At the end of the 1964–65 campaign, Andy Bathgate, who was a creative winger like Mahovlich, said: "Imlach never spoke to Frank Mahovlich or me for most of the season, and when he did, it was to criticize. Frank usually got the worst. We are athletes, not machines, and Frank is the type that needs some encouragement, a pat on the shoulder every so often." That outspoken observation was Bathgate's last as a Maple Leaf, but "The Big M" remained in Toronto for several more years.

Mahovlich sipped champagne from the Stanley Cup for a fourth time in 1967, before the Leafs made a blockbuster trade late in the following season that sent him to the Detroit Red Wings. The Maple Leaf Gardens switchboard was swamped with outraged callers, but for Mahovlich, "It was as if a piano had been lifted off my back." His production improved dramatically, and he hit a career high of 49 goals in 1968–69 on a line with Gordie Howe and Alex Delvecchio.

After two All-Star seasons, Mahovlich was traded to the Montreal Canadiens in 1971. "Hockey is fun again with this bunch," he admitted with a grin. "Even in practices, you can feel the Canadiens' love of sheer speed and what has become known as fire wagon hockey." Mahovlich jelled immediately with his new teammates and found the net 14 times in the spring of 1971 to set a playoff goal-scoring record and help the Canadiens win the Stanley Cup. He followed up with his two highest regular-season point totals on the way to Montreal's Stanley Cup victory in 1973, before he was lured back to Toronto. This time, however, it was to play for the Toronto Toros of the World Hockey Association.

Mahovlich spent four years in the WHA, the last couple with the Birmingham Bulls in Alabama, which made for a rather ignominious end to a Hall of Fame career. But the rewards have come. In 1998, Mahovlich—with his hockey celebrity his only obvious qualification—was appointed by Liberal Prime Minister Jean Chrétien to the Canadian Senate. He can hold the unelected position until age 75.

DATE OF BIRTH
Timmins, Ontario
January 10, 1938–

NHL CAREER
1956–74
Toronto, Detroit, Montreal

	GP	G	A	TP	PIM
RS	1181	533	570	1103	1056
PO	137	51	67	118	163

AWARDS
1st All-Star (3), 2nd All-Star (6), Calder,
Stanley Cup (6), HOF 1981

Dickie Moore

Dickie Moore was upset, wondering whether he was holding back his linemates by playing with a broken wrist. His centerman, Henri "The Pocket Rocket" Richard, looked as if he had a real shot at the 1957–58 Art Ross Trophy as scoring leader. On the other wing, the legendary Maurice "Rocket" Richard was still an offensive force and as fiery a personality as ever. When Moore offered to relinquish his spot on the line, Montreal coach Toe Blake called a meeting and asked the Richard brothers whether they wanted a change.

"We got here together," they quickly replied, "we end together." That vote of confidence, Moore believed, typified the attitude of the Montreal Canadiens in the 1950s. In the end, Moore did prevent Henri Richard from winning the scoring crown that year, but only because he took it home himself.

"A hockey player is not smart enough to think."

Three months with a specially designed cast helped Moore suit up for every match that season, and he missed surprisingly few games over his entire career, despite myriad other injuries. For all his formidable talent, Moore was fortunate even to have made it to the NHL. Two broken legs as a boy marked the beginning of a lifetime plagued with knee problems. Although hampered by numerous operations, separated shoulders and broken hands, wrists and collarbones, and more than the average number of stitches, bruises and sprains, Moore was never really stopped.

He followed up his Art Ross–winning campaign by setting a new record in defending his title the following year. His career-high 41 goals and 55 assists would not be beaten for seven seasons. Moore also made a huge contribution to six Stanley Cup victories for Montreal, including all five consecutive wins in the last half of the 1950s.

His team boasted eight future Hall of Fame members, and it took Moore some time to feel comfortable in that milieu. "It was like a nightmare for me as a young player," he admitted, "being around some of those great hockey players."

Moore had worked his way up through the Canadiens organization, but unwilling to sign for the NHL's minimum salary, Moore didn't join the parent club until Christmas 1951. He then scored an impressive 18 goals in the 33 games remaining in his rookie season with the Habs, but injuries restricted him to only 31 NHL games—and three goals—over the next two seasons. Healthy through the 1953 playoffs, he contributed three goals to Montreal's Stanley Cup win. He then led all scorers in postseason action the following year, aided by a record-breaking two-goal four-assist game.

"The worst thing that could happen to a hockey player is that he starts to think," Moore once said. "A hockey player is not smart enough to think." Yet an obvious intelligence added a dimension to his rugged approach to the game, and he resented the notion that he was uncontrolled. "I did anything I had to do to win and keep my job," he explained with self-awareness. "I had to play a certain style."

In 1962, Moore started an equipment-rental company, a venture that met with the disapproval of Canadiens' brass, who thought it would distract him from hockey. When Montreal initiated conversations about trading him in 1963, Moore quit hockey. "I couldn't think of playing for someone else," he claimed, although Toronto managed to lure him back to the NHL for the 1964–65 season, after one year of retirement. Still only 33 years old, Moore was restricted by injuries to 38 games, and his two goals and four assists convinced him that it was time to hang up his skates again.

When the league expanded in 1967, the St. Louis Blues persuaded Moore to come out of retirement one last time. Again limited by injuries, he played only 27 games but showed flashes of his former glory and helped his team to the Stanley Cup finals. While his team bowed out to Montreal in four straight games, Moore made his final exit with his head held high, distinguishing himself with seven goals and seven assists in 18 playoff games. In 1974, he was inducted into the Hockey Hall of Fame.

DATE OF BIRTH
Montreal, Quebec
January 6, 1931–

NHL CAREER
1951-63, 1964-65, 1967-68
Montreal, Toronto, St. Louis

	GP	G	A	TP	PIM
RS	719	261	347	608	652
PO	135	46	64	110	122

AWARDS
1st All-Star (2), 2nd All-Star, Ross (2),
Stanley Cup (6), HOF 1974

Maurice Richard

Rarely does a man gain mythic status while he is still alive, but early in his career, Maurice Richard transcended the role of folk hero. While the goals he battled for were on the rink, "The Rocket" seemed to personify many of the aspirations and frustrations of French Canada. Nothing illustrated that relationship so well as the explosive night of March 18, 1955, in what became known as "The Richard Riot."

Two days earlier, Richard had been involved in a stick-winging brawl. His explosive energy, best exemplified by his flashing black eyes, occasionally expressed itself in rage. Disarmed of his stick three times in a raucous melee, Richard committed the unpardonable sin of striking a linesman with his fist. NHL president Clarence Campbell suspended the Montreal star for the final few games of the season as well as the playoffs.

At the time, Richard was leading the NHL scoring race and the Canadiens were vying with the Detroit Red Wings for first place, so Montreal fans felt that the rug had been pulled out from under them. Campbell was the target of numerous threats, but he took his regular seat at the next Canadiens home game. On arrival, he was pelted with insults, eggs and debris. The Canadiens were soon losing to Detroit by a 4-1 margin, and the crowd grew angrier. Someone lit a tear-gas canister as the first period ended, and Campbell forfeited the match to Detroit.

"I had the same kind of determination from the time I was a boy of 7 or 8."

The enraged fans streamed out of the Montreal Forum, joining several thousand others outside who were demonstrating against Richard's suspension. An estimated 5,000 people then went on a rampage, smashing windows and looting stores in downtown Montreal. The next day, while shopkeepers cleaned up the mess, Richard went on the radio and appealed, successfully, for calm.

Many have argued that "The Richard Riot" was the dawn of Quebec's Quiet Revolution, signaling an end to French-Canadian tolerance of English-Canadian subjugation. Regardless, it was a defining moment for Richard, the Montreal Canadiens and the NHL. The Canadiens lost to Detroit in seven games in the Stanley Cup final that year but went on to win five consecutive Cups before "The Rocket" retired in 1960 and Montreal's remarkable streak ended.

Richard's record of 50 goals in 50 games, set during the 1944–45 season, stood until Mike Bossy equaled his achievement in 1981. Richard broke Nels Stewart's long-standing record of 325 regular-season goals and set a new high of 544 career goals before hanging up his skates. Yet he is best remembered for his playoff performances. Perhaps the ultimate clutch player, Richard scored six playoff overtime goals, still an NHL best. His 82 playoff tallies included 18 game-winners, four hat tricks, two four-goal games and a five-goal barrage against the Toronto Maple Leafs on March 23, 1944. In fact, he so dominated that game—a 5-1 Canadiens' victory—that he was chosen its first, second and third star.

Richard believed that there was only one thing that separated him from the rest: desire. "I had the same kind of determination from the time I was a boy of 7 or 8," he explained. "I wanted to win all the time, to score goals. That's all I had on my mind." Richard led the NHL in goals scored over five separate seasons but never won the Art Ross Trophy as scoring champion. Fittingly, the NHL inaugurated the Maurice "Rocket" Richard Trophy in 1999 to honor the regular-season goal-scoring leader. "For generations of hockey players and fans, 'The Rocket' was *the* goal scorer," declared NHL commissioner Gary Bettman. "His determination and skill symbolized the best the game has to offer."

Although Richard had a falling out with the Canadiens not long after he retired in 1960, he eventually patched things up and served the club as a goodwill ambassador for the last years of his life. Thousands of people—most of whom had never seen him play—lined the streets of Montreal to offer their final respects in May 2000.

DATE OF BIRTH
Montreal, Quebec
August 4, 1921–May 27, 2000

NHL CAREER
1942–60
Montreal

	GP	G	A	TP	PIM
RS	978	544	421	965	1285
PO	133	82	44	126	188

AWARDS

1st All-Star (8), 2nd All-Star (6), Hart,
Stanley Cup (8), HOF 1961

DATE OF BIRTH
Trencin, Czechoslovakia
February 14, 1982–

NHL CAREER
2000–04
Minnesota

Marian Gaborik

Marian Gaborik is clearly number one in Minnesota. A native of Trencin, Czechoslovakia, he was quickly embraced by fans in the northern U.S. state. Gaborik was the first draft pick ever for the Minnesota Wild, chosen third overall at the 2000 NHL entry draft. On October 6, 2000, he scored the first goal in franchise history. Playing under Minnesota coach Jacques Lemaire's "defense first" system would curb any sniper's output, but 18-year-old Gaborik managed to adopt his coach's approach while still tallying a team-leading 18 goals and an equal number of assists.

"Marian's not there yet, but he's improving," said Lemaire midway through Gaborik's rookie season. "His defense is day and night from where it was in training camp. "

Minnesota assistant coach Craig Ramsay was impressed by Gaborik, who successfully made the switch from left to right wing, amid a host of other changes. "He's got a goal scorer's hands," noted Ramsey. "He scores goals that you might say he was lucky—batting pucks out of the air, scoring on the backhand while going away from the net, and if he is tied up he finds ways to get his stick free so he can get a quick shot on net."

"He has the ability to cut through the trap like a knife through butter."

"I think he has all the skills to be something special," concurred Phoenix Coyotes coach Bobby Francis. "The thing that jumps out at me is his tremendous skating ability. Marian Gaborik has a beautiful stride, a very powerful stride. He has great hands and good vision on the ice that is quite remarkable for a player at such a young age. The first time we played Minnesota he did an end to end rush that reminded me of Gilbert Perreault. He has the ability to cut through the trap like a knife through butter."

Gaborik's 30 goals the following year were another team high. He credits his early training with the famed Dukla Trencin club for his NHL success. "In Slovakia, I was playing with all older guys and I tried to always work on my skills," said Gaborik. "Talent is one thing, but you have to continue to work hard. When you put it all together, good things happen."

Gaborik spent the first half of the 2002–03 season vying for the NHL scoring title. The Wild went on a similar tear. After an undefeated exhibition series, they continued to win consistently through the first half of the season. Gaborik was named Player of the Week in October, after posting six points in a 6-1 win over Phoenix. "Everything I touched either went in the net or went to a teammate who put it in the net," said Gaborik humbly. "It's a big honor. A lot of the credit has to go to my teammates." He finished the year with 30 goals and once again led the team with 65 points. More important, Minnesota made the playoffs for the first time.

"Every player put heart and soul into it," said Gaborik, after the Wild had overcome the Colorado Avalanche, defending Stanley Cup champions, in overtime in the seventh game of the 2003 Western Conference quarterfinals. Minnesota then vanquished the powerful Vancouver Canucks before finally falling to the Anaheim Mighty Ducks in the conference finals. Gaborik led the Wild with 17 points in 18 playoff games. With his contract up for renewal, he felt a large raise was in order.

A climate of austerity gripped the NHL in the summer of 2003, and the Minnesota Wild was already the lowest-spending team in the league. Gaborik's bid for a $6.5-million per season, three-year contract was flat-out rejected by Wild general manager Doug Risebrough, who proposed numbers approximately half that high. Gaborik switched agents midstream, trying to "inject new blood" and end the impasse, but the Wild entered the 2003–04 campaign without their career-leading scorer in the lineup. The two parties eventually found a middle ground. Look for Gaborik, one of the most exciting, talented and hard-working young wingers in hockey today, to star with the Wild for many years to come.

	GP	G	A	TP	PIM
RS	295	96	112	208	132
PO	18	9	8	17	6

DATE OF BIRTH
Freiburg, West Germany
January 21, 1981–

NHL CAREER
2001–04
Atlanta

Dany Heatley

Sadly, it is difficult to think about 23-year-old winger Dany Heatley today without remembering a deadly accident. On September 23, 2003, Heatley was driving an estimated 80 miles per hour when he lost control of his Ferrari and crashed into a brick wall. He suffered a concussion, broken jaw, torn knee ligaments and shoulder injuries. Tragically, his teammate and passenger Dan Snyder fared far worse.

After six days in a coma, Snyder succumbed to a massive head injury. Heatley's blood alcohol content was far below the legal limit, but the combination of speed and recklessness led to criminal charges (eventually settled with three years probation and a penalty of community service).

"Some players slow down when they get the puck. He speeds up."

June 24, 2000, was a far happier day. In Heatley's hometown of Calgary, Alberta, the Thrashers selected Heatley with the second overall pick in the NHL entry draft. The flashy winger had just concluded his first successful season with the University of Wisconsin after lighting up the Alberta Junior Hockey League the previous year with 70 goals and 126 points for the Calgary Canucks in 1998–99. He returned to Wisconsin in 2000–01 and tallied 24 goals and 33 assists in 39 games. At season's end, Heatley was voted both a First Team NCAA All-American and a finalist for the Hobey Baker Award as the top American college player.

In 2001–02, the Thrashers introduced Heatley to Atlanta along with Russian teenager Ilya Kovalchuk. Heatley maintains that what set the pair apart from other rookies was a healthy dose of self-confidence. "For Ilya and I, that came right off the bat. They played us together almost from the get-go and, after a couple of games, we were comfortable."

The two young guns made a strong impression around the league and vied for the lead in team scoring for most of their rookie season. Unlike Kovalchuk, however, Heatley earned praise for bringing more than offense to his game. "He can do it all," said teammate Yannick Tremblay. "Some players slow down when they get the puck. He speeds up. He can find a hole, shoot, you name it. He has been able to make a difference, right away, every time he's on the ice."

"There is no real set formula to what makes a guy successful at such a young age, but a key for those two guys in Atlanta is that they have free reign," observed Anaheim's Paul Kariya. "By that I mean if they make a mistake, they're right back on the ice. In a lot of cases guys are helped out by playing for expansion teams. You're likely not going to get a lot of shifts on a Stanley Cup contender."

Kovalchuk's season ended prematurely due to a separated shoulder, and Heatley finished atop all rookie scorers with 41 assists and 67 points. He won the Calder Trophy and was named to the 2002 NHL All-Rookie Team. His sophomore campaign was even more impressive. Heatley continued to win praise for his complete game while leading the team with 41 goals and 89 points. He was named MVP at the mid-season All-Star Game after potting a record-tying four goals and surpassing Wayne Gretzky as the youngest player to score an All-Star hat trick. At season's end, Heatley had cracked the NHL's top ten in scoring.

It took months of rehabilitation, but Heatley regained his NHL form late in the 2003–04 season and was named tournament MVP while winning a World Championship gold medal for Canada (for the second consecutive year). Then, in November 2004, only weeks after the courts decided the outcome of his car accident, the dark cloud that had hung over Heatley returned. Playing for a Swiss club during the NHL lockout, he took a puck in the face. Although he was wearing a visor, Heatley suffered a serious eye injury. But he was back on the ice a couple of months later, playing for a Russian squad, and suited up for Team Canada at the 2005 World Championships. Despite horrific setbacks, Dany Heatley's skills, fortitude and determination put him back on top.

	GP	G	A	TP	PIM	AWARDS
RS	190	80	101	181	132	Calder
PO	0	0	0	0	0	

DATE OF BIRTH
Stara Lubovna, Czechoslovakia
January 12, 1979–

NHL CAREER
1997–2004
Ottawa

94

Marian Hossa

Marian Hossa's hometown of Trencin, Slovakia, is a hockey hotbed that rivals some famed Canadian towns for exporting NHL stars. Its Dukla Trencin club boasts alumni Hossa, his younger brother, Marcel Hossa, Marian Gaborik, Miroslav Satan, Pavol Demitra and Zigmund Palffy, just to name some of the current NHL stars. The Ottawa Senators watched Marian Hossa score 25 goals and 19 assists in his last season for Dukla Trencin, and then selected him with their first pick in the 1997 NHL entry draft.

Eighteen-year-old Hossa started the 1997–98 campaign with Ottawa and earned third-star status in his first NHL game. After seven games, however, he was sent to spend the rest of the season with the Portland Winter Hawks of the junior Western Hockey League. He recorded 45 goals and 40 assists in 53 games there and earned WHL Rookie of the Year and First All-Star Team honors, as well as a spot on the Canadian Major Junior First All-Star Team. Unfortunately, in the last few minutes of the Memorial Cup finals, Hossa suffered a major knee injury that cost him a quarter of the next season.

"You have to have the strength if you're going to get to the net."

Hossa joined the Senators on December 5, 1998 and scored his first NHL goal four days later. He used his strength well along the boards and demonstrated impressive stickhandling ability, but was willing to barge through the opposition when circumstances dictated. He also adapted well to coach Jacques Martin's defensive system. After 60 games, Hossa not only had a strong plus-18, but he had also tallied 15 goals and 15 assists. He finished runner-up to Colorado's Chris Drury for the Calder Trophy and joined the NHL's 1999 All-Rookie Team.

"He definitely has a long career ahead of him and there's no doubt he's going to be a marquee player for this franchise," said teammate Daniel Alfredsson early in the 1999–2000 season. Hossa's confidence grew with every goal he scored and by season's end he was tied for the team lead with 29. His 27 assists put him third in Senator scoring, but it was a shot he took that *didn't* lead to a goal that really stood out.

On March 11, 2000, Hossa fired a puck at the Toronto net and his follow-through had tragic consequences; Hossa clipped Leaf defenseman Bryan Berard's eye with his stick. Berard suffered a cut cornea, detached retina and fractured orbital bone. The young rearguard's season—and almost his career—was ended, and Hossa felt sick with guilt. A private and public apology, and Berard's forgiveness, helped put the accident behind him.

Hossa challenged for the Rocket Richard Trophy for most of the 2002–03 campaign, but his scoring touch faded near the end of the season. "He's been generating some chances, but sometimes you just go through stretches like this in a season," noted Ottawa coach Jacques Martin. "Better now than in the playoffs." Hossa completed the campaign with a team-record 45 goals, fourth highest in the league. More important, he helped lift the Sens into first place in the regular season and, as Martin had hoped, regained his scoring touch in the post-season. Hossa notched 16 playoff points (5 goals, 11 assists in 18 games) before Ottawa fell to the New Jersey Devils in the Eastern Conference finals. The Devils went on to win the Stanley Cup championship.

Hossa spent the summer of 2003 working out with the intention of bulking up. Six-foot-one and 199 pounds the previous season, he tipped the scales at 208 pounds for 2003–04.

"You have to have the strength if you're going to get to the net," explained Hossa. "You can't just think you can go out there and score goals. You have to be able to win the battles as well."

"He's an individual that drives himself to make sure that he's at the top of his game," noted coach Martin appreciatively. "I think his commitment shows with the improvement we've seen in his strength and quickness. He's had success, but his work ethic hasn't dropped off. And, if you look at him, he's a team-oriented guy. He's always determined to come back and improve every year."

	GP	G	A	TP	PIM
RS	467	188	202	390	243
PO	51	13	21	34	18

DATE OF BIRTH
Tver, USSR
April 15, 1983–

NHL CAREER
2001–04
Atlanta

Ilya Kovalchuk

Ilya Kovalchuk wears sweater number 17 in honor of Valeri Kharlamov, one of Russia's greatest players. No matter that the man who starred for the Soviet Union in the 1970s died in a car crash in 1981, almost two years before Kovalchuk was born; the Kharlamov legend lives on, and so far the young Russian has not embarrassed himself by drawing comparisons.

Kovalchuk first attracted international attention at the 2000 World Under-17 Championships. He led Russia to the gold medal with a tournament-leading 14 points in six games, prompting the Hockey Hall of Fame to request his stick as a memento. Kovalchuk also impressed at subsequent Under-18, Under-20 and World Junior Championships.

Flashy and endlessly creative on the attack, Kovalchuk also has size. At six-foot-two and 235 pounds, he is strong and feisty with a good measure of cockiness. Add his blazing shot and excellent speed to the total, and it's easy to see why NHL clubs salivated at the thought of acquiring him. On June 23, 2001, the Atlanta Thrashers made 18-year-old Kovalchuk the first Russian player ever chosen as number one at the NHL entry draft.

"This kid could score with a nine-iron."

The Thrashers' second NHL season began with left-winger Kovalchuk on a line with 20-year-old right-winger Dany Heatley, the team's first pick in the 2000 entry draft. The promising youngsters didn't disappoint. Kovalchuk scored in his second NHL game and battled Heatley for months for 2001–02 rookie-of-the-year honors. At the 2002 Olympic Games, Kovalchuk scored a goal and two assists in six games for Russia, and on February 23 won an Olympic bronze medal.

His NHL season came to a sudden close on March 10 when he separated his shoulder in a game against the New York Islanders. Kovalchuk led all rookies with 29 goals at the time, and despite missing the last 16 games, his goal-scoring lead held up. Only Heatley, two points ahead when Kovalchuk got injured, finished the season with more than Kovalchuk's 51 points. In a close vote, Heatley edged Kovalchuk for the Calder Trophy.

When the 2002–03 season began, Thrashers coach Curt Fraser was hard pressed to get Kovalchuk to give more attention to defense. "No matter how many goals you score, you can't give up more," said Fraser after making Kovalchuk a healthy scratch in an October game. "He needs to learn that lesson now."

This wasn't the first time that Fraser couldn't get through to Kovalchuk. The previous season, he had instructed Kovalchuk—to no avail—to give up using illegally hooked blades. A week after Kovalchuk tallied six goals and earned MVP honors in the 2003 YoungStars Game on All-Star Weekend, the Edmonton Oilers requested a stick measurement. Kovalchuk's was confiscated and he served a two-minute penalty. He served his time, jumped out of the box, went in on a breakaway and scored; he then skated by the Edmonton bench, showed his new blade and taunted, "Is this stick okay?"

Unchastened, Kovalchuk was caught again in 2002–03. Again, he goaded his opponents, this time the Florida Panthers. However, the Panthers got the last laugh after scoring twice and beating the Thrashers. "If he's going to show us the blade, he'd better make sure he wins the game," chuckled Panther Peter Worrell.

"This kid could score with a nine-iron," added Fraser. "He doesn't need an illegal stick." The team's losing record cost Fraser his coaching job, but Kovalchuk's 38 goals and 29 assists in the 2002–03 season gained him a healthy measure of forgiveness.

Though Heatley bested Kovalchuk with a 41-goal, 48-assist 2002–03 campaign, his star was dimmed during Atlanta's 2003 training camp when he crashed his Ferrari, killing teammate Dan Snyder and badly injuring himself too. While the Thrashers pulled together as a family to deal with the tragedy, Kovalchuk took the team reins and led them to their best start ever. At season's end, he tied for the league lead with 41 goals and was named to the second All-Star Team.

"If I gave him any more ice time," said coach Bob Hartley, "I would have to put him in the net."

	GP	G	A	TP	PIM		AWARDS
RS	227	108	97	205	148		2nd All-Star, Richard
PO	0	0	0	0	0		

DATE OF BIRTH
Njurunda, Sweden
October 9, 1980–

NHL CAREER
2002–04
Detroit

Henrik Zetterberg

In Sweden, he is known simply as "Zata." Heralded by many as the best player not playing in the NHL in 2001–02, Henrik Zetterberg received a rare tribute for a 21-year-old hockey player. His club team, Timra IK, retired his jersey number 20 shortly after he was voted the Swedish Elite League's 2002 MVP. He'd earned the league's 2001 rookie of the year title with 46 points in 47 games the previous season, but Zetterberg had played for Timra IK teams since he was a boy. He capped his homeland career when he made the 2002 Swedish Olympic Team, and he was one of only a handful of non-NHL players to do so. Zetterberg went on to play for Sweden at the 2002 World Championships, making seven goals and five assists in eight games, and won a bronze medal.

The Detroit Red Wings made him the 210th player chosen in the seventh round of the 1999 NHL entry draft. "If they want me or have room, I will go," said Zetterberg. "We will have to sit down and have a discussion after the World Championship to see what they say. I hope I am going to play there next year." Detroit seems to unveil an excellent youngster every season, and in 2002–03, that was Zetterberg.

"You can feel comfortable using him in any situation."

At just under six feet tall and 190 pounds, and not the speediest player on the ice, Zetterberg makes up with flair what he lacks in sheer physicality. He is an amazing stickhandler and his creative dekes frequently make the highlight reels. He sees the ice well and makes great passes. But Zetterberg plays a decent defense as well, and earned only eight penalty minutes while playing 79 games in his rookie season. Overall, he made the transition to the NHL look relatively easy, without spending any time in Detroit's farm system.

"People who see him regularly can appreciate all the things he does on the ice to help us win games," said Detroit coach Dave Lewis. "You can feel comfortable using him in any situation."

For most of his rookie year, Zetterberg played left wing alongside 24-year-old center Pavel Datsyuk and 38-year-old right-winger Brett Hull. "We think the same on the ice," observed Zetterberg. The unlikely combination—tagged the "Two Kids and a Goat" line—proved potent, especially for sniper Hull. He potted 37 goals and added 39 assists; Datsyuk had 12 goals and 39 helpers and Zetterberg led all rookies with 22 goals and 22 assists. Detroit finished first in the Western Conference and Zetterberg eagerly anticipated his first taste of Stanley Cup playoff competition.

Unfortunately, the Red Wings were swept in the first round by Anaheim. In a close vote for the Calder Trophy, Zetterberg finished second to St. Louis defenseman Barret Jackman, and was named to the 2003 All-Rookie Team.

The Red Wings lost centermen Sergei Fedorov and Igor Larionov to free agency in the summer of 2003, and their other center, captain Steve Yzerman, was not in top form after spending most of the previous season recovering from major knee surgery. The team looked to their impressive winger for a solution. "It's not that big of an adjustment," claimed Zetterberg, on being moved into the position he grew up playing. "If they want me to stay at center, that'll be fine with me."

Zetterberg started the first game of the 2003–04 campaign on the top line between veterans Brendan Shanahan and Ray Whitney. But after two games, coach Lewis had him back on the wing with Datsyuk and Hull. Zetterberg is unfazed by the shuffling. "I'd say 90 percent of my career, I've played center," explains Zetterberg. "But it really doesn't matter that much. I was happy on the wing last season. As a player, you go out there and do the best you can do. I want to play well and help this team win."

He suffered a broken leg twelve games into the season, but Zetterberg made a speedy recovery and was back in the lineup a week before Christmas. Whether he plays the wing or center, or alternates between the two, Zetterberg is a versatile player the Red Wings can count on.

	GP	G	A	TP	PIM
RS	140	37	50	87	22
PO	16	3	2	5	4

The Defensemen

The Defensemen

The defenseman's primary responsibility is to protect his goal from attack. He is allowed tremendous liberty in aggressively harassing opponents, especially in the slot—the critical area of ice in front of the net between the face-off circles—and generally, only the most blatant bludgeoning or tackling is penalized. For this reason, size and strength have traditionally been major factors in determining which players are assigned to the blue line. To achieve the status of the players in this position's upper echelon, though, it's important to contribute offensively as well.

Bobby Orr literally revolutionized defense, but finesse has always had its place, and the rushing defenseman harks back to the game's earliest days. King Clancy and Eddie Shore flamboyantly carried the puck up-ice in the 1920s and 1930s, and many pundits credit years of fine play by fleet-footed Red Kelly with inspiring the creation of the James Norris Memorial Trophy in 1953. Awarded annually to the NHL's defenseman showing "the greatest all-around ability," the Norris Trophy went to Kelly in its inaugural year but was then dominated by strong puck-handlers Doug Harvey and Pierre Pilote, who were both in or near the twilight of their Hall of Fame careers when Orr burst onto the NHL scene in 1966. What Orr did, however, was take a blue-liner's offensive prowess to a previously unimagined level.

Instead of following the norm and generally dishing the puck off after bringing it into the opponents' end, Orr routinely carried it right to the net, breaking the 30- and 40-goal marks by a defenseman for the first time and winning two scoring championships. But blocking shots and guarding the front of his own net after scampering back into position if his team failed to score were also intrinsic to Orr's game. "I'm glad I won the award now," said Harry Howell presciently after being presented with the 1967 Norris Trophy, "because I expect it's going to belong to Bobby Orr from now on." For the following eight consecutive years, Orr did indeed win the Norris, which has likewise gone almost unfailingly to a player cast in his image ever since. Rod Langway—a stay-at-home defensive stalwart for the Washington Capitals in the 1980s—stands as the only exception to date.

Brad Park and Denis Potvin typified the breed of rugged and offensively talented defenseman most highly sought after once Orr had shown what was possible. Having one of the team's principal scoring threats patrolling the blue line soon became an expectation rather than an anomaly. Three-time Norris winners Paul Coffey and Chris Chelios and five-time victor Ray Bourque have reinforced the standard for premier blue-liners, but the young defensemen featured here have not posted impressive offensive statistics yet. While hitting, particularly the open-ice body check, seems to be a dying art, a more one-dimensional player such as Barret Jackman or Jiri Fischer *can* still emerge as one of the league's better rearguards by superbly taking care of business in his own end. The position, after all, is still called defense.

LEGENDS

Raymond Bourque

Chris Chelios

King Clancy

Dit Clapper

Paul Coffey

Doug Harvey

Tim Horton

Red Kelly

Bobby Orr

Brad Park

Pierre Pilote

Denis Potvin

Larry Robinson

Serge Savard

Eddie Shore

YOUNG LIONS

Jay Bouwmeester

Eric Brewer

Jiri Fischer

Barret Jackman

Robyn Regehr

Opposite: In the twilight of his career, Buffalo Sabres defenseman Tim Horton (2) guards the net with fellow rearguard Jim Schoenfeld (6) and goalie Roger Crozier. Previous page: New York Islander Denis Potvin (5) helps out his netminder Billy Smith.

Raymond Bourque

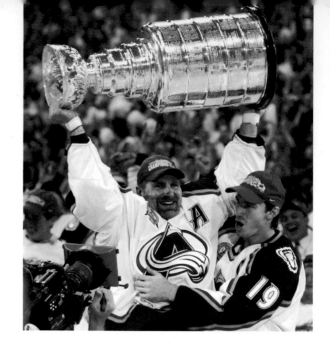

On October 11, 1979—just before his first NHL game—Raymond Bourque was handed sweater number 7. He was naïve enough not to fathom the implications of donning Phil Esposito's old number; fortunately for Bourque, his success was immediate, and he didn't have to suffer the heckling most rookies wearing a legend's number would have faced. Bourque was awarded the Calder Trophy and earned First All-Star Team status. Number 7 seemed to suit him just fine.

It wasn't really an issue for anyone until 1987, when the Bruins decided to honor Esposito by "retiring" his number, although the club said that Bourque could continue to wear what had become "his" number. Bourque had great respect for all that Esposito had done for the Bruins, so a secret plan was hatched. On "Phil Esposito Night," in front of a sellout crowd in the intimate Boston Garden, Bourque stripped off his number 7 jersey and handed it to Esposito. The retired star was visibly moved when Bourque then turned and showed the crowd his new number, 77. Bourque used 77 for the rest of his career.

"A Stanley Cup would be unbelievable."

Bourque was virtually a fixture at the NHL All-Star Game throughout his career. But the 1996 All-Star Game, held in Boston, stands up as a career highlight. With only 37 seconds remaining in the third period, Bourque snared the puck and rifled in the winning goal. The hometown crowd erupted with joy, much more for the goal scorer than for the victory. The lengthy ovation was renewed when Bourque was named the game's most valuable player. The other players seemed almost as pleased as Bourque himself.

Bourque's official All-Star selection at the end of his rookie year was the first of a record 17 consecutive nominations. His five Norris Trophies rank behind only Doug Harvey and Bobby Orr. He was also runner-up to the league's best defenseman six times, including in 2000–01 when he was 40 years old. He finished his career holding numerous NHL scoring records: most career points by a defenseman (1,579), most career goals by a defenseman (410), most career assists by a defenseman (1,169), most years in playoffs (21) and most career playoff assists by a defenseman (139). Part of the secret to Bourque's success was that he took nothing for granted, even after clinching a future spot in the Hockey Hall of Fame. "I love playing the game," he explained. "That's why I'm doing well. I'm still looking at it like a little kid. Every day, you've got to prove yourself, and that's how I've played this game my whole career."

Bourque went to the Stanley Cup finals twice with Boston and both times led all defensemen in playoff scoring. Unfortunately the Bruins fell easily to the Edmonton Oilers on each occasion. "A Stanley Cup," said Bourque, "would be unbelievable," but he seemed fated to join a small number of illustrious players who never saw their names engraved on the Cup. After years of denying an interest in playing anywhere else, Bourque finally requested a trade to a contender after almost 21 seasons as a Bruin. He was dealt to Colorado in March 2000.

His first playoffs with the Avalanche were disappointing, but his new team dedicated their 2000–01 campaign to getting Bourque a ring. They accomplished their mission, and captain Joe Sakic gave a tearful Bourque the privilege of being the first on the team to hoist the Cup. Bourque announced his retirement the following summer. The Avalanche lifted his number 77 into the rafters the following season, as did the Bruins. Fittingly, Phil Esposito was on hand in Boston to hand Bourque his retired sweater.

DATE OF BIRTH
Montreal, Quebec
December 28, 1960–

NHL CAREER
1979–2001
Boston, Colorado

	GP	G	A	TP	PIM
RS	1612	410	1169	1579	1141
PO	214	41	139	180	171

AWARDS

1st All-Star (12), 2nd All-Star (6), Calder,
Norris (5), Clancy, Stanley Cup, HOF 2004

Chris Chelios

After emigrating from Greece to the United States in 1951, Gus Chelios developed a passion for hockey and his hometown Chicago Blackhawks that he passed on to his children. "It's that pit-bull upbringing," his son Chris once joked. "They grow 'em tough in those small European countries, and I've got this temper that gets me into trouble now and then." But Chris Chelios also managed to channel some of that ferocity into stardom in the NHL.

Chelios then spent two seasons at the University of Wisconsin and a year with the American national team. After he played at the 1984 Olympic Games, Montreal was ready for him. He played the remainder of the 1983–84 campaign and six more seasons with the Canadiens, highlighted by a Stanley Cup championship in 1986. "Those were great years," he recalled. "I listened and learned a lot. Playing for the Canadiens is like getting a Harvard law degree. Montreal players know what it's like to win." Chelios was awarded the Norris Trophy as the NHL's finest defenseman in 1989, 1993 and 1996.

"I liked going out there and being the guy people hate to play against."

Chelios grew as a player, but his penalty minutes also increased. "I was a real pain in my first 8 or 10 years in the league," he has confessed. "I liked going out there and being the guy people hate to play against. I thought I was more effective being mean and getting at their top players." Yet all too often, Chelios took a bad penalty. After the Canadiens made a quick exit in the 1990 playoffs, Chelios was traded to the Blackhawks for the flashy little centerman Denis Savard.

Savard had been a crowd favorite in the Windy City, and the trade for Chelios initially was an unpopular move. But Chelios quickly endeared himself to the Chicago fans. He played a nasty game, accumulating career-high penalty time in his first three seasons as a Blackhawk, with 192, 245 and 282 minutes, respectively.

"I'm going to have to find a line between being mean and taking penalties," Chelios remarked after serving a suspension in 1994, and he has been somewhat successful. "I'm trying to control myself more now," he said more recently. "I don't want to be known as the type of player who is constantly in trouble. I want to show I can play aggressively and be mean but not jeopardize the team's success." Team success with Chicago was fleeting at best, although Chelios's play remained stellar.

"He was hard-working and down to earth in high school, and he's still like that today," said Frank Kiszka, the hockey moderator at Mount Carmel High School, where Chelios played for two years. "He's still very much 'South Side.' "

Rather than test the free-agent waters in 1997, Chelios signed a contract extension committing him to Chicago until age 38, for a salary less than market value—a move that struck many as a breath of fresh air. "Money doesn't motivate me," claimed Chelios. "I play hockey because I love it, and I was fortunate enough to go back home and have my whole family together again. . . . To me, it's a great honor to play in the NHL, and especially for the Blackhawks."

Sadly, Chelios' loyalty wasn't reciprocated; Chicago traded him to Detroit in March 1999. Chelios flourished as a Red Wing, although he missed most of the 2000–01 campaign due to a knee injury. After recovering, Chelios joined the First All-Star Team (his seventh All-Star berth), and was runner-up for the Norris Trophy. He capped his stellar season by helping Detroit win the Stanley Cup. Chelios is truly a champion for the ages.

DATE OF BIRTH
Chicago, Illinois
January 25, 1962–

NHL CAREER
1984–2004
Montreal, Chicago, Detroit

	GP	G	A	TP	PIM
RS	1395	178	736	914	2695
PO	222	30	107	137	378

AWARDS
1st All-Star (5), 2nd All-Star (2), Norris (3),
Stanley Cup (2)

King Clancy

At first, Frank Clancy's nickname was an inside joke. His father, an Ottawa sports celebrity with a reputation for toughness, had earned the royal designation "King of the Heelers" back in the 1890s for his ability to "heel" the ball out of a football scrum. Only an 18-year-old, 127-pound sprite when he first approached the Ottawa Senators in 1921, the junior "King" earned a spot on the defending Stanley Cup champion Ottawa roster because of his spirit and fleetness. Signed as a substitute player, Clancy saw little ice time for a couple of years except in practice.

"They wanted me on their team, and the only opening was on defense," said Clancy. "I had to take it or leave it, and I took it." He didn't get his first real chance until the 1923 Stanley Cup finals against the Western Canada Hockey League champion Edmonton Eskimos. In the final game of a two-game total-goals playoff, injuries knocked out two defensemen, and Clancy substituted admirably. Then he spelled Hall of Fame center Frank Nighbor and both wingers in turn. In those days, no substitution was allowed for a penalized goalie, so when Ottawa goaltender Clint Benedict took a penalty, Clancy went between the pipes. He didn't allow a goal and even raced up the ice with Benedict's big goalie stick for a shot on net. Ottawa won the Cup, and Clancy was hailed as the team's hero.

"I had to take it or leave it, and I took it."

Clancy became a regular in 1923–24. In 1927, he helped Ottawa win another Stanley Cup, and in the 1929–30 season, he led all NHL defensemen in scoring, with a career-high 17 goals and 23 assists, before being traded to the Toronto Maple Leafs for the then-exorbitant sum of $35,000 and two players. Toronto's owner Conn Smythe was looking for someone to fill the building he planned to construct for the start of the 1931–32 season, and Clancy didn't disappoint him. He led the Leafs to their first Stanley Cup victory in the spring of 1932 in the new Maple Leaf Gardens, before capacity crowds.

Clancy earned All-Star Team honors in his first four seasons with Toronto, but he combined his hockey prowess with clownlike theatrics. He once provoked Boston's notorious Eddie Shore into dropping his gloves, then shook Shore's hand enthusiastically while grinning and said, "Good evening, Eddie. How are you tonight?" Everyone, including Shore, was left laughing. Although Clancy engaged in plenty of fights over the years, he didn't make many lasting enemies.

The Leafs decided to honor Clancy on St. Patrick's Day, 1934, and the ceremony culminated in the presentation of the guest of honor dressed as Old King Cole. When the lights were momentarily extinguished, Clancy doffed a big white beard, regal robes and a crown to reveal himself garbed in a brilliant emerald-green uniform. He remained decked out in green when the game began, but the visiting New York Rangers gave Clancy such a rough time that he donned his Maple Leafs' blue-and-white for the second and third periods.

After playing only six games for Toronto in the 1936–37 season, Clancy hung up his skates—briefly. He coached the Montreal Maroons for half a season before NHL president Frank Calder asked him to switch to refereeing. "I suppose Mr. Calder figured out I knew a lot about the rule book," Clancy said, "after having spent so much time sitting and thinking in the penalty box."

Clancy retained his sense of humor in his new position of authority, and he was tolerant. "If at all possible, I avoided giving misconduct penalties," he said. "If a youngster blew his top, I quietly told him to keep cool or he would hurt his team. If an older player became abusive, I found that it helped to give him a second chance. So I would look tough and say, 'Just repeat what you said.' Usually, [the player] took the warning and skated away."

Clancy coached the Leafs in the mid-1950s and again in 1972, but he served the Leafs best as an unofficial goodwill ambassador until his death in 1986. The NHL established the King Clancy Memorial Trophy in 1988, which is awarded annually to the player who best exemplifies leadership both on and off the ice while making a significant humanitarian contribution to his community.

DATE OF BIRTH
Ottawa, Ontario
February 25, 1903–November 10, 1986

NHL CAREER
1921–37
Ottawa, Toronto

	GP	G	A	TP	PIM
RS	592	137	143	280	904
PO	61	9	8	17	92

AWARDS
1st All-Star (2), 2nd All-Star (2),
Stanley Cup (3), HOF 1958

Dit Clapper

Dit Clapper unintentionally coined his own nickname as a child. Called "Vic" by his parents, the toddler could only say "Dit," and soon, that's how he was known to everyone. Playing all his games for the Boston Bruins, Clapper became hockey's first 20-year man, setting the NHL longevity record. Coincidentally, Clapper's last season was Gordie Howe's first.

After Howe had established himself in the league, he admitted to one ambition—to play for 20 years, "just like Clapper." While he eventually lasted even longer than Boston's wonder, Howe was unable to challenge Clapper's other distinction in the history books. A right-winger for his first 11 years in the league, Clapper hit even greater heights on the blue line. He remains the only NHL player to be awarded All-Star status both as a forward and as a defenseman.

"Clapper asked the referee to repeat himself. When he did, Clapper decked him."

Clapper joined Boston in 1927 at the age of 19. In his first two campaigns, he scored only 4 and 9 goals, respectively, but the Bruins won the Stanley Cup in 1929. The following season was different: Clapper erupted with 41 goals and 20 assists in what was only a 44-game season, good for third in the NHL scoring race. His performance was well deserving of an All-Star berth, but the NHL didn't begin honoring its elite in that manner until the 1930–31 season. Clapper was the NHL's Second All-Star Team's right-winger for the next two seasons and was named team captain in 1932–33.

At six-foot-two and 200 pounds, Clapper had a size advantage over most NHL players and the strength to match. No pacifist, he nonetheless didn't play the Boston-style roughhouse as defined by bruising defensemen Lionel Hitchman and Eddie Shore. He was even known to break up fights on occasion, although once he reached his boiling point, he was capable of inflicting heavy damage with his fists. One such punch almost got him into severe trouble.

Avenging a butt-end administered to a Boston rookie in the 1936 playoffs, Clapper was punching the offending Montreal Maroons player when the referee yanked him back by the hair. That was the referee's first mistake, for Clapper took great pride in his meticulously combed jet-black hair with the razor-sharp part. The young official then further enraged Clapper by denigrating his mother. Stunned by the comment, Clapper asked the referee to repeat himself. When he did, Clapper decked him.

The referee was Clarence Campbell, who 10 years later would become president of the NHL. Knowing Clapper's character and recognizing the role he himself had played, Campbell made a public apology and explained the circumstances to league president Frank Calder. Instead of receiving a lengthy suspension, Clapper was fined $100.

After 11 years at right wing, Clapper moved back to defense. At the end of the season, Clapper joined Shore as 1938–39's First All-Star Team defensemen. The two rearguards were an important part of Boston's Stanley Cup victory that spring. Clapper made the First All-Star Team the next two years as well.

Boston's 1940–41 team emerged as one of the strongest in NHL history. Clapper was runner-up in Hart Trophy voting to teammate Bill Cowley, and the Bruins swept Detroit in the Stanley Cup finals. Clapper won a Second All-Star Team spot in 1943–44. In addition to retaining him as captain, Boston's general manager Art Ross relinquished his coaching responsibilities and appointed Clapper player/coach for the 1945–46 campaign.

Clapper filled the role for a little more than two years before hanging up his skates and moving into coaching full-time. After almost three seasons behind the bench, though, Clapper had had enough. "Being a coach is a lousy job," he said in a surprise resignation speech on April 1, 1949. "I couldn't abuse these players. They're my friends."

Clapper had been inducted into the Hockey Hall of Fame the day after he retired from active play, and his number 5 jersey was raised to the rafters of the Boston Garden almost as quickly. Having reached hockey's pinnacles, Clapper severed his ties to the professional game, moved back to Canada and opened a sporting-goods store.

DATE OF BIRTH
Newmarket, Ontario
February 9, 1907–January 21, 1978

NHL CAREER
1927–46
Toronto

	GP	G	A	TP	PIM	AWARDS
RS	833	228	246	474	462	1st All-Star (3), 2nd All-Star (3),
PO	86	13	17	30	50	Stanley Cup (3), HOF 1947

Paul Coffey

When Paul Coffey emerged as an offensive star in the early 1980s, he drew inevitable comparisons to superstar Bobby Orr. But he bore that heavy burden of expectation successfully.

Frank Mahovlich made a huge impression on Coffey's father, and as a boy, Paul was coaxed to emulate "The Big M" and make every stride as long and strong as possible. "I would never have become a hockey player," he once admitted, "but for my father." Coffey's fluid and graceful style led many to remark that he could glide faster than most players could skate.

Playing for Glen Sather on the Edmonton Oilers added a further dimension to his game. Sather noted his rookie's speed and coaxed Coffey to jump up into the play more often. "I'd never done that before," said Coffey, "even in junior." The results were dramatic. As the fourth man in the rush, Coffey was a key to the Oilers' offense—not only did he skate fast, he was also capable of making a sterling setup or finishing a play with his accurate shot.

"I would never have become a hockey player but for my father."

After a decent rookie year, with 9 goals and 23 assists, Coffey almost tripled his offensive production with an 89-point sophomore season in 1981–82 and made either the First or Second All-Star Team for each of the next five seasons. His point totals continued to climb as he helped the franchise win its first two Stanley Cups, in 1984 and 1985. His stellar play, which included 12 goals and 25 assists in the 1985 playoffs, led many to believe that he should have won the Conn Smythe Trophy that year, but Wayne Gretzky, who had amassed 10 more points, won the award. Coffey peaked offensively with a record-breaking 48-goal, 90-assist campaign in 1985–86 and won his second consecutive Norris Trophy, but the Oilers were eliminated in the second round of the playoffs. The team rebounded to win the Cup again the next year, but in the midst of the celebrations, Coffey dropped a bombshell: His days as an Edmonton Oiler were over.

Coffey felt denigrated by Edmonton owner Peter Pocklington when he sought to renegotiate his contract, and was adamant that he wouldn't play for "Peter Puck" again. He was traded to the Pittsburgh Penguins in the 1987. Mario Lemieux was the perfect receiver for the long-bomb passes for which Coffey was famous. In 1991, Lemieux got the Stanley Cup ring he coveted, and Coffey earned his fourth, but while the Penguins were en route to their second consecutive Cup, Coffey was traded to the Los Angeles Kings.

"Hockey's a funny game," Coffey has observed. "You have to prove yourself every shift, every game." Despite all that he had done, Coffey hadn't always received his due.

In his 1988 autobiography, Larry Robinson had high regard for Coffey: "Coffey has the uncanny ability to make a defensive play in his own end and start the puck back the other way before the other team can react," and opined that Coffey was "probably the best player in hockey today when it comes to the transition game."

Dealt to Detroit in January 1993, Coffey won his third Norris Trophy in 1995 as a Red Wing. The remainder of his career was less successful. Unhappy with his 1996 trade to Hartford, Coffey was dealt to Philadelphia after 20 games with the hapless Whalers. After two seasons with the Flyers, he made brief stays in Chicago, Carolina and Boston before retiring in the summer of 2001.

When Coffey hung up his skates, his 1,135 career assists and 1,531 points placed him fourth and ninth, respectively, in the NHL record book.

DATE OF BIRTH
Weston, Ontario
June 1, 1961–

NHL CAREER
1980–2001
Edmonton, Pittsburgh, Los Angeles, Detroit, Hartford, Philadelphia, Chicago, Carolina, Boston

	GP	G	A	TP	PIM
RS	1409	396	1135	1531	1802
PO	194	59	137	196	264

AWARDS
1st All-Star (4), 2nd All-Star (4),
Norris (3), Stanley Cup (4), HOF 2004

113

Doug Harvey

Few kings have fallen further from grace than Doug Harvey, who died in 1989 at the age of 65 in a Montreal hospital after living for several impoverished years on the fringes of society. At his peak, Harvey had ruled the NHL blue line for more than a dozen years, winning the Norris Trophy as the league's best defenseman seven out of eight seasons between 1955 and 1962. Diagnosed late in life with manic-depressive disorder, his death from cirrhosis was the predictable result of years of using alcohol to deal with his wild mood swings. Although he had quit drinking three years before his death, the damage to his liver was irreversible.

Harvey was one of the smartest players ever to lace on skates, but he wasn't always appreciated. His deliberate and efficient manner initially struck many as lackadaisical. Instead of racing up and down the ice, Harvey moved methodically, breaking up opposition rushes with an economical poke-check or coolly intercepting a pass when it looked as if he were out of position. He'd keep the puck on his stick while almost motionless, then just before the opposition stripped him of it, he'd flick a beautiful pass. Nor was Harvey averse to carrying the puck in front of his own net. Such hockey heresy gave management fits until they realized that his apparently reckless and lazy maneuvers were actually planned and executed almost perfectly.

His age and lifestyle were starting to catch up with him.

Harvey had the ability to dictate play. Often referred to as the team's "quarterback," he could slow a game's pace by corralling the puck and shepherding his team up the ice, or he could ignite the action by snapping long lead passes to a fleet of sharpshooters. The combination was so deadly on the power play, with Montreal exploding for two or three goals in a two-minute span, that the league changed the rules in 1956 to allow a penalized player back on the ice as soon as his team was scored upon.

Harvey was such an integral part of Montreal's dynasty in the 1950s that in 1957, when he teamed up with Detroit's Ted Lindsay in a failed attempt to form a Players' Association, the Canadiens refused to "exile" their star defenseman to the lowly Chicago Blackhawks, as some clubs had done to other association supporters. Harvey was a leader both on the ice and in the dressing room, where his sense of humor and lighthearted approach made him the life of every party. While this endeared him to his teammates, Montreal management eventually decided that he was more trouble than he was worth and traded him in 1961.

In 1961–62, Harvey joined the New York Rangers as player/coach, and even with his additional responsibilities, he won his seventh Norris Trophy and got the sad-sack Rangers into the playoffs. Missing being "one of the boys," however, Harvey relinquished his coaching duties the following season.

Harvey continued to play, but while his mental skills were still sharp, his age and lifestyle were starting to catch up with him. Early in the 1963–64 season with the Rangers, he was demoted to the minors, where he bounced around for five years with a number of teams. With the NHL expansion in 1967 he returned to the NHL and he joined the St. Louis Blues for the 1967–68 playoffs, chipping in four assists, and played for them the following season at the age of 44. He then scouted professionally, but before long, he had worked himself out of hockey altogether, gathering notice for a few days only when news of his fatal illness and subsequent death was broadcast.

DATE OF BIRTH
Montreal, Quebec
December 19, 1924–December 26, 1989

NHL CAREER
1947–64, 1966–9
Montreal, NY Rangers, Detroit, St. Louis

	GP	G	A	TP	PIM
RS	1113	88	452	540	1216
PO	137	8	64	72	152

AWARDS

1st All-Star (10), 2nd All-Star,
Norris (7), Stanley Cup (6), HOF 1973

Tim Horton

Tim Horton's name lives on through the chain of coffee and donut shops he founded, but regrettably few patrons remember the outstanding hockey player who launched the business. Horton was recognized as an NHL All-Star six times and was runner-up in Norris Trophy voting twice, the second time when he was 39 years old. Generally acknowledged as the strongest man in the game while he was playing, Horton skated through most of 24 NHL seasons. "There were defensemen you had to fear because they were vicious and would slam you into the boards from behind," declared Bobby Hull, perhaps the only player in the league more muscular than Horton. "But you respected Horton because he didn't need that type of intimidation. He used his tremendous strength and talent to keep you in check."

"If he'd only get angry," King Clancy once lamented, "no one would top him in this league." But Horton believed that he had taken too many penalties early in his career because of his "hot temper."

"Maybe it's just a bad habit I've acquired. I like to play hockey."

Rather than punching back at an angry opponent, he'd envelop his foe in a crushing bear hug. Derek Sanderson once bit Horton during a fight; years later, Horton's widow, Lori, asked him why. "Well," Sanderson replied, "I felt one rib go, and I felt another rib go, so I just had to get out of there!" Horton accumulated 518 points over his lengthy career, a huge total in his day. Even though he reportedly measured a couple of inches less than his official five-foot-ten, Horton was a menacing sight as he crossed the opposition blue line with his almost fully erect skating style and the momentum of a freight train.

In 1955, defenseman Bill Gadsby caught Horton on a rare occasion when his head was down with "the hardest check in my life." Horton suffered a broken leg and jaw, the worst of a litany of injuries suffered over the years. Horton's daughters begged him to let his crew cut grow longer in the 1970s, not so much to keep up with the day's fashion but to hide his numerous scars. Yet injuries and age seemed to be little more than minor inconveniences to Horton.

His "retirement" was an almost routine event at contract-renewal time, but when the Leafs fired Punch Imlach, who liked to prolong and resurrect older players' careers, the 39-year-old Horton declared, "If this team doesn't want Imlach, I guess it doesn't want me."

Toronto owner Harold Ballard asked Horton later in the summer of 1969 whether he'd consider playing again for more money. "If somebody said they'd double my salary," Horton joked, "I might consider it." Ballard took him up on his jest, and Horton went from $45,000 to $90,000 a season. Yet the Leafs dealt Horton to the New York Rangers late in the 1969–70 season.

Horton retired after his second year with the Rangers, but his old teammate Red Kelly convinced him to play a year for him in Pittsburgh. Although Horton's business partner wanted him to focus on the donut business, Imlach talked Horton into joining his new club, the Buffalo Sabres, in 1972. "Maybe it's just a bad habit I've acquired," Horton joked. "I like to play hockey. I have a long time ahead of me to sit behind a desk."

In negotiating what proved to be Horton's final contract, Imlach, to his lasting regret, gave Horton the car of his choice as part of his compensation. A lifelong automobile enthusiast, Horton chose a Ford Pantera—a sports car capable of dangerously high speeds. Horton was killed instantly in a single-vehicle accident in 1974 while returning home to Buffalo from a game where, fittingly, he had been named third star in Maple Leaf Gardens.

DATE OF BIRTH
Cochrane, Ontario
January 12, 1930–February 21, 1974

NHL CAREER
1952–74
Toronto, NY Rangers, Pittsburgh, Buffalo

	GP	G	A	TP	PIM
RS	1446	115	403	518	1611
PO	126	11	39	50	183

AWARDS
1st All-Star (3), 2nd All-Star (3),
Stanley Cup (4), HOF 1977

Red Kelly

Red Kelly was the last defenseman to win the Lady Byng Trophy. In the early 1950s, he made the award almost a personal possession by winning it three out of four years and coming second in the other. "Kelly is as good a player as I've seen in my long connection with hockey, which dates back to 1906," said Montreal manager Frank Selke Sr., in 1952. "More than that, he exemplifies everything that is desirable in a young man, and the Detroit club is fortunate to have a man of his integrity and character in its lineup."

Kelly was tough—he won a welterweight boxing championship during his junior days at St. Mike's in Toronto. Looking back at his hockey career, Kelly recalled: "I had some good fights with some tough players. But I also knew that fighting hurts the hands and takes you off the ice."

Fleet of foot and creative with the puck, Kelly was a league All-Star for eight consecutive seasons and the first winner of the Norris Trophy in 1953–54. Yet the red-haired defender remained an offensive threat; he led NHL defensemen in goals eight times. His role in Detroit's four Stanley Cup wins in the 1950s is often forgotten, but Kelly was a critical component of a powerhouse club. He played up to 55 minutes a game, leading many to believe that he would quickly burn out, but he was indefatigable and lasted 20 years in the NHL.

"I thought that the greatest stickhandlers were in hockey, but I found out they were in Parliament."

Early in 1960, Kelly was prodded into revealing that the Red Wings had coaxed him into playing on a broken ankle during the previous season. General manager Jack Adams immediately traded him to the New York Rangers. Kelly refused to report, and began a life outside the game. An exploratory call from King Clancy and the Toronto Maple Leafs 10 days later proved fruitful, and a new deal was swung. But the Leafs weren't looking for a defenseman.

"One year, Sid Abel got hurt in the playoffs," said Kelly, "and they moved me to center between Howe and Lindsay. I believe I also lost a First All-Star selection one year because of helping out on the forward line. The voters didn't know where to put me." With Kelly as his centerman in 1960–61, Frank Mahovlich finally realized his potential, netting 48 goals. Kelly had his first 20-goal season and 50 helpers, with a paltry 12 minutes in penalties, to earn his fourth and final Lady Byng Trophy.

While center Kelly helped the Leafs win the Stanley Cup four out of the next six years, he also served as a Member of Parliament for his Toronto riding, commuting to Ottawa for four seasons. He was elected twice but finally gave up his second job to focus on the game. "I thought that the greatest stickhandlers were in hockey," he said after retiring from elected office, "but I found out they were in Parliament."

After hoisting the Stanley Cup in his last season, the 40-year-old Kelly retired from active play as the record-holder for most career playoff games, at 164. He coached the Los Angeles Kings in 1967–68 for their inaugural season. Two years later, he joined the Pittsburgh Penguins for several seasons before returning to Toronto to coach.

Kelly guided the Leafs for four complete seasons, and is fondly remembered in Toronto for his introduction of "Pyramid Power," a positive-thinking campaign. Kelly had pyramids under the bench and in the dressing room and provided smaller ones for his players to sleep with. The novelty eventually wore off—Toronto lost to Philadelphia in the quarter-finals for three successive years—and Kelly retired from the game after the 1976–77 season.

DATE OF BIRTH
Simcoe, Ontario
July 9, 1927–

NHL CAREER
1947–67
Detroit, Toronto

	GP	G	A	TP	PIM
RS	1316	281	542	823	327
PO	164	33	59	92	51

AWARDS
1st All-Star (6), 2nd All-Star (2), Norris,
Byng (4), Stanley Cup (8), HOF 1969

Bobby Orr

Doug Orr was one of the speediest hockey players ever seen in Parry Sound, Ontario, and he had a young son with tremendous potential. He thought that his boy Bobby should play forward; after all, Bobby was fast on his skates, could stickhandle like the devil and had a hard shot and a deft scoring touch.

Fortunately for hockey, Bucko McDonald—a standout NHL defenseman in the 1930s and 1940s—was head coach of all the Parry Sound boys' teams and felt that Bobby should play defense, maintaining that he was a natural at the position. "Bucko taught me almost everything I know," Orr later declared graciously.

"It wasn't hard," McDonald confessed, "because even at that age, you could see that Bobby was special." The little defenseman soon came to the attention of the Boston Bruins, who did everything they could to ensure that Orr became, and remained, their exclusive property.

"Losing Bobby was the biggest blow the NHL has ever suffered."

In deference to Orr's youth, Boston made exceptional arrangements to allow him to play for the Oshawa Generals of Ontario's junior league in 1962. The 14-year-old Orr continued to live at home, 150 miles from Oshawa, and was driven to every game. He didn't practice with the team once, yet at season's end, he was selected to the Second All-Star Team.

Orr dominated junior hockey for three more years. When he finally made his Boston debut in 1966, the hockey prodigy lived up to his advance billing—and more.

Orr's 13 goals and 41 points in his first NHL campaign may seem humble, but only Chicago's Pierre Pilote tallied more as a defenseman that season. Orr won the Calder Trophy as the NHL's outstanding rookie and a Second All-Star Team selection.

While most teams had included at least one rushing defenseman since Eddie Shore's day, Orr took the concept to another level. His radical approach to the game invited argument, including the one Bucko McDonald had won years earlier. "We played him at center for six or seven games in his rookie year," said Harry Sinden, Orr's first coach in Boston. "He was only tremendous. On defense, he was phenomenal."

Orr went on to set offensive records, twice winning the Art Ross Trophy as the NHL's leading scorer and finishing as runner-up to teammate Phil Esposito three times. In 1970–71, Orr set the high mark for assists and total points by a defenseman, with 37 goals and 102 assists, a record that still stands.

Orr won the Norris Trophy for eight consecutive years. He blocked shots and cleared the front of his net, and dropped his gloves when the situation called for it. But his lasting legacy is the way he spearheaded the attack. "One of his great gifts," noted the analytical Eddie Shore, "is the ability to gauge precisely the speed of the man he is passing to."

Orr's 1970 goal to win Boston's first Stanley Cup in 29 years is remembered best—his hands raised in celebration as he is hoisted in the air by St. Louis defenseman Noel Picard. Derek Sanderson, who fed him the puck that day, commented: "We had the one player who could finish a play like that."

"Winning the Cup twice was great," Orr told *The Hockey News*, "but I wonder why we didn't win it more often." Due in part to his betrayal at the hands of his now disgraced agent Alan Eagleson, Orr regretfully forsook Boston to sign a free-agent contract with the Chicago Blackhawks in June 1976. But his greatest disappointment was his forced early retirement. Plagued by knee injuries throughout his career (he even sat out all of 1977–78 to recover), Orr was finished at the age of 30. He played fewer than 10 seasons, but left an indelible mark on the game. "Losing Bobby," said Gordie Howe, "was the biggest blow the NHL has ever suffered."

DATE OF BIRTH
Parry Sound, Ontario
March 20, 1948–

NHL CAREER
1966–78
Boston, Chicago

	GP	G	A	TP	PIM	AWARDS
RS	657	270	645	915	953	1st All-Star (8), 2nd All-Star, Calder, Hart (3), Ross (2),
PO	74	26	66	92	107	Norris (8), Smythe (2), Stanley Cup (2), HOF 1979

Brad Park

When he negotiated his son's first NHL contract, Brad Park's father got a verbal agreement from New York Rangers general manager Emile Francis that Brad would be paired with defenseman Harry Howell, a 16-year NHL veteran. "I knew that I could learn a lot by watching Harry," said Park, "but he really went out of his way to work with me. I learned so many little things just in the four weeks I spent in my first Rangers training camp. Most of them were mental aspects of the game—how to foresee or deal with different situations." By his second season, Park was a league All-Star, a status he upheld for seven of the next 10 years.

Park played a rugged, hard-hitting game and became the team's "policeman." He fought a lot yet his point totals continued to rise along with his penalty minutes. The Rangers made it to the Stanley Cup finals in 1972 before losing to the Boston Bruins in a six-game battle. "Bobby Orr was the difference," said Park, who finished runner-up to Orr in Norris Trophy voting that season for the third time in a row.

After Park led his team in assists (57) and points (82) in 1973–74, he lost out to Orr again. "For a while, I guess, I was trying to compete with him," admitted Park that year. The self-assured Park allowed that he might be slightly better defensively than his rival but that Orr's speed allowed him to make mistakes and still get back into position. "But let's face it," Park added, "there's only one Bobby Orr. From now on, I'm just going to be Brad Park."

"I took over a last-place team, and I kept them there."

Park was named team captain for the 1974–75 season, but early the following year, Rangers management deemed a shake-up necessary. Park, Jean Ratelle and Joe Zanussi were sent to archrival Boston in return for Phil Esposito and Carol Vadnais. On record as hating both Boston and the Bruins' fans, Park couldn't have been less pleased. There was a silver lining, though: He would be playing with Bobby Orr.

Boston coach Don Cherry decided that his two blue-line stars would spell each other so that one would be on the ice at all times, but they would man the power play together. Park described their efficiency in converting the manpower advantage into goals as "about 50 percent"; unfortunately, the combination lasted for only 10 games before Orr's knees gave out.

"[Coach] Don Cherry asked me to sit back and concentrate on the defensive side of the game," said Park, "unless I was on the power play or we were behind late in the game. Many wondered if I had lost a step." Cherry later speculated that his instructions cost Park a Norris Trophy—he came second behind Denis Potvin twice—but noted that he probably helped prolong a Hall of Fame career at the same time. Although Park underwent nine operations on his left knee, he didn't miss a season or the Stanley Cup playoffs for 17 years. He went to the finals twice with the Bruins, but a championship was just not in the cards.

A free agent in 1983, Park finished his playing career in Detroit, where he finally got his name on some NHL hardware in 1984: the Bill Masterton Trophy in recognition of his perseverance and dedication to hockey. His subsequent coaching career in Detroit was short. "I took over a last-place team," said Park, "and I kept them there." He was fired after 45 games. Park was deeply involved in legal action against NHL owners for salary collusion in the 1970s. The suit was eventually dismissed when it was ruled the statute of limitations had run out.

DATE OF BIRTH
Toronto, Ontario
July 6, 1948–

NHL CAREER
1968–85
NY Rangers, Boston, Detroit

	GP	G	A	TP	PIM	AWARDS
RS	1113	213	683	896	1429	1st All-Star (5), 2nd All-Star (2),
PO	161	35	90	125	217	Masterton, HOF 1988

Pierre Pilote

"My first pair of skates was my mother's," said Pierre Pilote, "and I didn't play organized hockey until I was 17." From such humble beginnings arose one of the NHL's premier defensemen. Pilote won the Norris Trophy three years in a row and sandwiched those victories with three second-place finishes. A successful rushing defenseman in the NHL's "Original Six" era, Pilote was honored as an NHL All-Star for eight consecutive years, five in a row on the First Team. That Pilote's name is not as celebrated as some who accomplished less may owe as much to the nasty side of his game as it does to his team's relative lack of success. For back then, if you weren't a Chicago Blackhawks fan, you probably *hated* Pilote.

"When penalties came, I always made sure I got my money's worth," confessed Pilote. "The guy paid for it, whether it was from boarding or charging, and I saw that as a sign that I was in the game." A definite part of his strategy was intimidation, a technique he first honed as a teenager. After moving to Fort Erie, Ontario, from Kenogami, Quebec, he started to play industrial-league hockey. "You'd call it a butcher league now," claimed Pilote. He once joked that the first English words he learned were "Do you want to fight?"

"When penalties came, I always made sure I got my money's worth."

In 1952–53, Pilote joined the Buffalo Bisons of the American Hockey League. He apprenticed for over three years under player/coach Frank Eddolls, a former NHL defenseman. "Frank taught me that the game was simple and uncomplicated, if you played it right," said Pilote. "The short pass rather than the long rink-wide kind was the key to movement, the key to the attack." Pilote got his first call-up to the Blackhawks in 1955–56, and by the next year, he was there to stay.

Although only five-foot-nine and 180 pounds, Pilote played with determination and an obvious mean streak. He pulled no punches when clearing the front of his net. Yet he had a light touch in moving the puck, either by passing or by skating it up-ice, and he steadily refined every facet of his emerging skills.

By the 1959–60 season, he was the NHL's leading scorer among defensemen, with 7 goals and 38 assists, and was named to the Second All-Star Team. The following season, Pilote led the league with 165 penalty minutes and made a major contribution to Chicago's greatest success in the past 65 years—and counting. In the spring of 1961, he tied Gordie Howe for the most playoff points, with 3 goals and 12 helpers, including assists on three game-winners in the finals, and the Blackhawks defeated the Red Wings for their first Stanley Cup victory in 23 years.

A pioneer in the use of visualization, Pilote spent hours analyzing his own play and that of his teammates and opponents and imagining possible situations on the ice. "Tommy Ivan [Chicago's general manager] once told me I could see things other players couldn't," said Pilote, but his quick reactions and uncanny anticipation came both from his mental practice and from continuous hard work. He also set high personal goals for himself. Pilote won his first Norris Trophy in 1962–63, and the next season, he recorded 46 assists, tying an NHL best. In 1964–65, he broke Babe Pratt's record of 57 points by a defenseman, set in the 1943–44 season, with 14 goals and 45 assists.

Pilote was still team captain when Chicago traded him to Toronto in the summer of 1968. His subsequent season's total of 46 penalty minutes with Toronto was a career low, a sign that some of the edge was gone from his game. Pilote decided that it was time to retire. He was elected to the Hockey Hall of Fame in 1975.

DATE OF BIRTH
Kenogami, Quebec
December 11, 1931–

NHL CAREER
1955–69
Chicago, Toronto

	GP	G	A	TP	PIM
RS	890	80	418	498	1251
PO	86	8	53	61	102

AWARDS
1st All-Star (5), 2nd All-Star (3),
Norris (3), Stanley Cup, HOF 1975

Denis Potvin

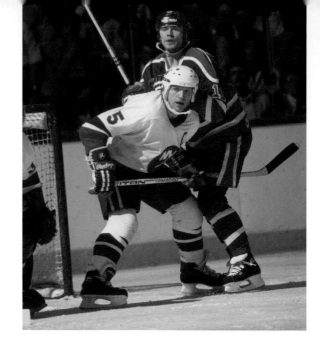

A precocious child, bigger and stronger than others his age, Denis Potvin had a temperament that would make him one of the most intimidating defensemen in NHL history. "I didn't want to become known as a bully," he recalled, "yet I had a fanatical obsession with being the best." At the age of 13, he joined his 17-year-old brother Jean's junior team, the Ottawa 67s, and made an immediate impression. "Potvin Touted as Next Bobby Orr" was the headline of the day and the next decade.

Potvin first experienced the pleasures of hitting in football and discovered that he could have that feeling on the ice too. "I found a similar thrill going into the corners, feeling the crunch of body against body, stick against stick," he said. "In a purely impersonal sense, I enjoyed hurting people with my body, as long as they weren't seriously injured."

"I enjoyed hurting people with my body, as long as they weren't seriously injured."

Leo Boivin, one of the most devastating body checkers in NHL history, coached Potvin for his last year of junior eligibility and helped him fine-tune his hip-checking technique—a dying art. But Potvin was frustrated. NHL rules then strictly prohibited players under the age of 20. Nevertheless, with 123 points in 1972–73, Potvin beat Bobby Orr's record and set a new mark for junior defensemen that lasted for 16 seasons. "Orr does things I don't do, and I do things he doesn't do," he said confidently. "You can't compare us."

The last-place New York Islanders selected Potvin as their first pick in the 1973 entry draft. "Now that I'm here," said Potvin, "I ask myself, What am I going to do next? Well, I want to be the best. I set my goals high. It keeps you working; it keeps you alive." He won rookie-of-the-year honors and was named the Islanders team captain in the fall of 1979.

"We know we can beat the Rangers," Potvin said when entering the 1975 playoffs against the Islanders' crosstown rivals. "We're younger, stronger, better. For some reason, though, we have too much respect for them. We treat them like gods." His team then proceeded to sweep the Rangers out of the playoffs. Potvin's first selection as First All-Star Team defenseman coincided with Orr's last.

Potvin later admitted that the confidence he displayed was a "security blanket," masking a deep-seated fear of failure. He hit the 30-goal mark late in his third season—a magic number for a defenseman that only Orr had reached—and he almost collapsed with relief. "I skated to the bench," recalled Potvin, "fell to the wooden plank and bawled as quietly as I could before 14,865 friends." He won the Norris Trophy, ending Orr's eight-year monopoly.

In the 1976 Canada Cup tournament that fall, Potvin led the international meet in points and in the plus/minus category, but Orr received the award as most valuable player. "Is Bobby Orr only going to have to play to be known as the best defenseman?" he fumed in a candid diary he kept for a Canadian magazine. But he gradually received more of the respect he craved.

"Potvin could hurt you in so many ways," said Islanders coach Al Arbour, "with a defensive play or a pass or a goal from the point. He also had a mean streak, so he could hurt with his stick or just physically, with his body." While Potvin won two more Norris Trophies during the 1970s, he felt hobbled by Arbour, who had been a "defensive defenseman" for 16 NHL seasons. But Potvin's all-around game was a key to the Islanders' four consecutive Stanley Cup wins in the 1980s.

On his own terms, Potvin retired in 1988, holding the records for the most goals, assists and points by an NHL defenseman.

DATE OF BIRTH
Ottawa, Ontario
October 29, 1953–

NHL CAREER
1973–88
NY Islanders

	GP	G	A	TP	PIM
RS	1060	310	742	1052	1354
PO	185	56	108	164	253

AWARDS

1st All-Star (5), 2nd All-Star (2), Calder, Norris (3), Stanley Cup (4), HOF 1991

Larry Robinson

Larry Robinson's selection at the 1971 NHL entry draft was not a big story at the time. Montreal made Guy Lafleur its first prize, although general manager Sam Pollock had a pocketful of extra picks, typically hornswoggled from NHL expansion teams. Robinson was the Habs' fourth choice. But "Big Bird" Robinson, gangly and tough, and "The Flower" Lafleur, smooth and graceful, would soon represent the careful balance of yet another Montreal team dynasty. Before that day came, however, each would have to serve an apprenticeship.

Lafleur joined "Les Canadiens" immediately and struggled in the limelight for a time, but Robinson was sent to the Nova Scotia Voyageurs for seasoning. Arriving at his first professional training camp at 193 pounds, Robinson, who was six-foot-four, was told that he had work to do. With effort, he played most of his career between 215 and 220 pounds.

Robinson was called up to Montreal midway through the 1972–73 campaign. Although the Canadiens tried to break him in gently, the rookie defenseman was able to sip champagne from the Stanley Cup for the first time that spring.

His reputation was forged, and he rarely had to brandish his fists again.

Concentrating on the defensive side of his game, Robinson cleared the front of his net with authority. He accumulated his highest penalty totals in his first two complete NHL seasons, partly through the mistakes that any young defenseman makes but also by establishing a presence. It took several more years before he really settled in to the kind of game he enjoyed most: hard-hitting but clean. After Robinson took apart the Philadelphia Flyers' notorious pugilist Dave "The Hammer" Shultz in the 1976 Stanley Cup finals, his reputation was forged, and he rarely had to brandish his fists again.

The Canadiens won four consecutive championships (1976–79), and Robinson, Serge Savard and Guy Lapointe— Montreal's trio of All-Star defensemen known as "The Big Three"— were key contributors. Robinson emerged as an offensive threat as well as one of "the trees in front of the net" that Boston coach Don Cherry cited as key to Montreal's domination of the Bruins in the Stanley Cup playoffs. While his main asset was his passing, Robinson often surprised opposing teams by using his size and long reach to carry the puck right to the goalmouth.

He won the first of two Norris Trophies as the NHL's premier defender, and the first of five consecutive All-Star Team selections with a career-high 19 goals and 66 assists, over the 1976–77 season. In the spring of 1978, Robinson notched 4 goals and 17 assists, tying regular-season scoring-champion Guy Lafleur for most playoff points, and won the Conn Smythe Trophy. In 1986, he won his sixth Stanley Cup ring with another All-Star season under his belt. Then, in 1989, after 17 years in Montreal, it was time for a change.

Robinson concluded his Hall of Fame playing career after three seasons with the Los Angeles Kings, with 20 consecutive playoff appearances on the record books. He was lured back into the NHL as assistant coach of the New Jersey Devils, who won the Stanley Cup in 1995. He then took the head coaching job with Los Angeles for four seasons before rejoining the Devils as an assistant in 1999–2000.

In a stunning move, Robinson was promoted to head coach with only eight games left in the season. He guided the team to another Cup win. When the team faltered in 2001–02, Robinson accepted a demotion back to assistant coach. He had his name etched on the Stanley Cup for the ninth time when New Jersey won again in 2003.

DATE OF BIRTH
Winchester, Ontario
June 2, 1951–

NHL CAREER
1972–92
Montreal, Los Angeles

	GP	G	A	TP	PIM
RS	1384	208	750	958	793
PO	227	28	116	144	211

AWARDS

1st All-Star (3), 2nd All-Star (3), Norris (2), Smythe, Stanley Cup (6), HOF 1995

Serge Savard

Broadcaster Danny Gallivan, who loved a colorful phrase, dubbed one of hockey's most deceptive maneuvers the "Savardian Spinarama." While other legendary defensemen, such as Doug Harvey and Bobby Orr, occasionally used the move, Serge Savard made it his own with regular success. "Savard would skate up the right-wing boards out of our zone," recalled teammate Larry Robinson, "usually right at an oncoming winger. Just as both reached the vicinity of the blue line, Serge would spin around 360 degrees and skate away from the checker. He'd perfected the move in both directions, clockwise and counterclockwise. Teams that sent in one or two forecheckers were reluctant to get too close to Serge, because he'd burn them."

"This is not only a victory for the Canadiens, it is a victory for hockey."

It took years of practice before Savard made such an audacious gambit in game situations, but his poise on the blue line was evident early in his career. After a two-game call-up in 1966–67, he joined the Canadiens on a full-time basis the following season. He contributed two playoff goals, despite seeing only spot postseason duty in Montreal's Stanley Cup victory. Then, in his second NHL season, he was awarded the Conn Smythe Trophy when the Canadiens successfully defended the Stanley Cup. Appropriate to his subsequent Hall of Fame career, Savard received the award as most valuable player not for some uncharacteristic heroics but for his solid two-way play. That was to be the individual hallmark for an astonishingly undecorated standout defenseman.

A broken leg cost Savard his place on the Stanley Cup-winning team of 1970–71. He broke his leg again the following year, and it looked as if he might be too brittle for NHL action. But he came back, played the last 23 games of the season and playoffs and missed very little action for the rest of the decade.

Savard was chosen as a member of Team Canada in the famous Summit Series in September 1972. He didn't play in the entire eight-game showdown between Canada's NHL professionals and the Soviet Union's national team, but he never dressed for a losing game either—the only Canadian player with that distinction.

Savard, Larry Robinson and Guy Lapointe, became known as "The Big Three" and were as powerful a blue-line triumvirate as hockey has ever seen. The Canadiens won four consecutive Stanley Cups, but wresting the crown from Philadelphia's "Broad Street Bullies" in 1976 was particularly sweet for Savard. "This is not only a victory for the Canadiens," claimed Savard, "it is a victory for hockey. I hope this era of intimidation and violence that is hurting our national sport is coming to an end. Young people have seen that a team can play electrifying, fascinating hockey while still behaving like gentlemen."

Savard received his only All-Star nomination for his 1978–79 season, the year he was also awarded the Bill Masterton Trophy—for perseverance, sportsmanship and dedication. The NHL wasn't alone in finally acknowledging Savard's distinguished career. Montreal made him team captain, an honor he held for two seasons until announcing his retirement. His old teammate John Ferguson had other ideas for him, though. Then general manager of the Winnipeg Jets, Ferguson picked up Savard for a $2,500 waiver fee and convinced him to play two more seasons for him.

Long known as "The Senator" by his teammates, because of the three-piece suits he often wore, Savard made an easy transition to the business world. And in 1983, he became the Montreal Canadiens' managing director, a post he held for 12 years.

DATE OF BIRTH
Montreal, Quebec
January 22, 1946–

NHL CAREER
1967–83
Montreal, Winnipeg

	GP	G	A	TP	PIM
RS	1040	106	333	439	592
PO	130	19	49	68	88

AWARDS
2nd All-Star, Smythe, Masterton,
Stanley Cup (7), HOF 1986

Eddie Shore

They called him the "Edmonton Express" and "Mr. Hockey"—until that title was usurped by a more modern legend named Gordie Howe—but "Old Blood and Guts" remains this defenseman's most apt epithet. Over the course of his career, Eddie Shore took 978 stitches to his body. His nose was broken 14 times and his jaw five, and he lost every tooth in his head. His back was fractured, his hip broken and his collarbone cracked. His eyes were frequently blackened, and he suffered cuts to the eyeballs. And every wound dramatically embellished Shore's reputation as the toughest player in hockey. Several wild seasons as a minor-league professional earned Shore an invitation to the Boston Bruins' training camp in 1926. Veteran tough-guy Billy Coutu took an immediate dislike to the newcomer and, in a bull-like rush down the ice, slammed into the significantly smaller Shore at full speed. Coutu hit the ice semiconscious, while Shore remained standing, his left ear split from top to bottom and blood gushing onto his face.

"Studying with Shore was like getting your doctorate in hockey science."

When the Bruins' doctor warned Shore that his ear would have to be amputated, Shore found someone willing to stitch up the wound instead. Shore kept his ear, and Boston had a player to be reckoned with.

He played his first NHL game on November 16, 1926, and finished the season with 12 goals—second among NHL defensemen. His penalty totals of 130 minutes were second in the league. He followed up his rookie campaign with a total of 165 penalty minutes (an NHL record that lasted for seven years) and 11 goals, tops for defensemen that 1927–28 season.

Shore had become a dynamic skater, with a low crouch and a long, flowing stride. He was as hard-hitting as ever, but his stickhandling made him a constant offensive threat as well. At the end of the 1930–31 season, Shore was named to the NHL's First All-Star Team, as he was six times after that. For the 1933–34 season, however, he was selected only to the Second All-Star Team, probably the result of his 16-game suspension for hitting Ace Bailey from behind at full speed on December 12, 1933. Shore himself suffered a head injury when Toronto's Red Horner dropped him to the ice with an uppercut even as Bailey writhed on the ice—Shore wore a helmet for the rest of his playing career.

But the incident brought Bailey's hockey career to an end and also left an indelible black mark on Shore's Hall of Fame career.

Shore won four Hart Trophies in the 1930s as the league's most valuable player. But after leading his team to a Stanley Cup victory in the spring of 1939, he made the bold decision to buy the Springfield Indians of the International Hockey League. As a result, Shore's NHL contract was traded to the New York Americans, where he agreed to play all their games and as many games for Springfield as he could.

That 1939–40 season was Shore's last in the NHL. He played one more season for Springfield before moving into management full-time, where he quickly became notorious for his penny-pinching and bizarre training methods. He "cured" goaltender Don Simmons of falling to the ice by tying his arms to the crossbar; he also introduced tap dancing in the dressing room and ballet steps on the ice to "improve balance, the foundation of an athlete's ability." When he died in 1985, Shore made sports headlines one last time, with colorful obituaries. Former player Kent Douglas claimed that "studying with Shore was like getting your doctorate in hockey science," yet for each flattering comment, there were several more stories highlighting his eccentricities and meanness.

DATE OF BIRTH
Fort Qu'Appelle, Saskatchewan
November 25, 1902–March 17, 1985

NHL CAREER
1926–40
Boston, NY Americans

	GP	G	A	TP	PIM
RS	550	105	179	284	1037
PO	55	6	13	19	179

AWARDS
1st All-Star (7), 2nd All-Star, Hart (4),
Stanley Cup (2), HOF 1947

DATE OF BIRTH
Edmonton, Alberta
September 27, 1983–

NHL CAREER
2002–04
Florida

Jay Bouwmeester

Befitting his large size, Jay Bouwmeester entered the NHL with a big splash. For months, Bouwmeester was slated by most scouts to be picked first in the league's 2002 entry draft. Two eleventh-hour trades changed that. For about 20 minutes the shy young man, along with the rest of the hockey world, didn't know what was happening. "There was nothing I could do about it, so I just watched how things unfolded," said Bouwmeester. "It's all part of the excitement, I guess." The Florida Panthers sent their prized first pick to Columbus, who took winger Rick Nash. Atlanta, choosing second, also ignored Bouwmeester and selected Finnish goaltender Kari Lehtonen. Later, the Thrashers announced that Florida had given them a couple of draft picks to guarantee they left Bouwmeester alone. Using the third pick they had received from Atlanta, the Panthers selected Bouwmeester, the player they had always coveted.

"When you're with Jay, it's like you've got your own room on the road."

"Jay would have been the number-one pick overall if we'd kept that pick," said Florida coach Mike Keenan. Bouwmeester lived up to his coach's high opinion of him over the course of his 2002–03 rookie campaign. Showing surprising poise, he played dependably in a league that welcomes only a handful of 19-year-olds in a season. Bouwmeester has always been mature beyond his years; he remains one of only four Canadians to play in the World Junior Championships at the age of 16.

Bouwmeester, tall and lanky, doesn't play an overly physical game, his greatest asset. "Jay is the best skater for his size I've seen," said Hall-of-Famer and Panthers broadcaster Denis Potvin. His transitional play, a required skill in today's NHL, is excellent. His superior vision and intuitive feel for the game—knowing when to hang back or join the rush, and recovering quickly when he makes the wrong decision—will only improve with more experience.

Bouwmeester honed his skills over four seasons as a junior with Medicine Hat in the Western Hockey League. The Edmonton, Alberta, native made the WHL's First All-Star Team, averaging a point a game with 11 goals and 50 assists in 2001–02. Most observers agree that Bouwmeester showed more offensive potential than his results in the NHL indicated. He potted four goals and added a dozen helpers in his rookie year. More impressively, he played in all 82 regular-season games. Bouwmeester became the Panthers' number-one defenseman when the rebuilding Panthers traded Sandis Ozolinsh to Anaheim in March 2003. "Congratulations, your rookie season has just ended after 52 games," said Keenan, a man better known for brutal candor than humor. By season's end, Bouwmeester was averaging 20 minutes a game against the opposition's top lines. His minus-29 cost him votes for the Calder Trophy (he placed seventh) but Bouwmeester made the 2003 All-Rookie Team alongside Barret Jackman of the St. Louis Blues. Bouwmeester also earned an invitation to join Team Canada for the 2003 World Championships. The youngest member on the team, he was voted the tournament's top defenseman; he also came home with a gold medal around his neck. Yet Bouwmeester remains genuinely humble and remarkably soft-spoken, almost to a fault.

"When you're with Jay, it's like you've got your own room on the road," joked Panther teammate Lance Ward. "The kid is so quiet, he tiptoes to the bathroom at night. I look over and I'm not sure he's breathing."

"If anything, he maybe has to work on being a little more cocky... or maybe confident's the word," agrees Denis Potvin. Bouwmeester has also been encouraged to get stronger. A harder edge will undoubtedly come to Bouwmeester's play too; Bouwmeester tallied only 14 penalty minutes as a rookie, and 30 minutes as a sophomore. But Bouwmeester is no diamond in the rough. He's already a star, and a huge part of the future for the Florida franchise.

	GP	G	A	TP	PIM
RS	143	6	30	36	44
PO	0	0	0	0	0

DATE OF BIRTH
Vernon, British Columbia
April 17, 1979–

NHL CAREER
1998–2004
NY Islanders, Edmonton

Eric Brewer

The 2000–01 season marked defenseman Eric Brewer's NHL breakout. Only 21 years old, he played with increasing confidence and skill, finishing the season second on the Oilers in hits, and fifth in shots blocked. Brewer's offensive talents had also improved. At season's end, he had seven goals, 14 assists and a tie for the team lead with a plus-15. He added a goal and five assists in six playoff games. Brewer earned an invitation to join Team Canada for the World Championships in Germany and played well on the larger European ice surface.

He'd come a long way from his beginnings in the league. The New York Islanders had had high hopes for Brewer and selected him with the fifth pick in the 1997 NHL entry draft. Brewer spent one more junior season with the Prince George Cougars in the Western Hockey League before entering the NHL at age 19. Brewer played 63 games as a rookie, scoring five goals and six assists, with an acceptable minus-14, considering the Isles finished the 1998–99 season well out of the playoffs with only 58 points.

> ## "He makes some mistakes but nobody's ever played a perfect game. Gordie Howe made mistakes too."

His team completed an almost identical sad-sack campaign in 1999–2000, and Brewer's season was even more disappointing. After three games, the Islanders demoted him to Lowell in the American Hockey League. Brewer returned to the Islanders a couple of weeks later but broke a toe after playing eight games. He missed a half-dozen contests due to the injury, then played 15 games for New York before being reassigned to the minors to finish out the season.

Isles general manager Mike Milbury has a reputation for giving up on highly touted prospects too early. Eric Brewer is but one example. On June 24, 2000, Milbury sent Brewer, big winger Josh Green and a second-round draft pick to Edmonton for defenseman Roman Hamrlik. The change in scenery seemed to be just what Brewer needed, and that season he blossomed.

As talk about the 2002 Canadian Olympic team began in earnest, Brewer's name came up time and again. Perhaps only the humble British Columbia native was bowled over when he appeared on the 23-man roster unveiled in December 2001. "To me he was a no-brainer," said Team Canada general manager Wayne Gretzky. "He's got tremendous upside. He plays with emotion, he's tough; he can skate and jump into the play.

"He makes some mistakes but nobody's ever played a perfect game," added The Great One. "Gordie Howe made mistakes too." "It's almost a fairy tale," mused a jubilant Brewer at the end of the Nagano tournament. He'd not only taken a regular shift on the veteran-laden Canadian squad, but he had also notched a game-winning goal. "I've never won a World Juniors or a Memorial Cup or a World Championship or a Stanley Cup, so to come home with a gold medal is an amazing feeling." Then, at the 2002 World Championships held in Sweden later that spring, he tied for the team lead in scoring, with five points in seven games. To no one's surprise, Brewer got a hefty raise when he signed a new two-year contract with the Oilers.

"I don't think he was given an opportunity to develop in those first couple of years in New York," offered St. Louis' star rearguard Chris Pronger, speculating on how Brewer had improved so much so quickly. "He got into a situation in Edmonton where he could kind of sit back and be the fifth or sixth guy for the first 20 or 30 games and learn. Having time to do that definitely helps."

"The thing about Brew is he has the whole package," praises Edmonton coach Craig MacTavish. "He has the tools and the toolbox, as they say in hockey lingo. I don't think I've seen a defenseman who can skate like that. And he's really coming on. He's so much better now at picking the holes. Before, he had the raw ability but didn't know the path to take. Now he does." Few will be surprised if that path eventually leads to a Norris Trophy.

	GP	G	A	TP	PIM
RS	404	34	79	113	262
PO	12	2	8	10	8

DATE OF BIRTH
Horovice, Czechoslovakia
July 31, 1980–

NHL CAREER
1999–2004
Detroit

Jiri Fischer

His team has been known for its preponderance of veterans but young Jiri Fischer is an important member of the Detroit Red Wings. The Wings selected the Czech rearguard 25th overall in 1998, after his first season with the Hull Olympiques of the Quebec Major Junior League. Just shy of his eighteenth birthday, Fischer was already an impressive six-foot-five and 210 pounds with excellent skating ability and an aggressive edge. But the powerful Wings, fresh off back-to-back Stanley Cup victories, sent him back to Hull for seasoning.

Fischer made the league's First All-Star Team in 1998–99 with 22 goals, 56 assists and 141 penalty minutes. The following season, he stuck with the Wings.

"I think he's almost the complete package," said Detroit general manager Ken Holland. "He's got a good shot. He passes. He's physical. I think as he gets stronger, knows the league, he can play even more physical." But it took Fischer time to earn a regular spot in the lineup.

"I'll just be waiting for my opportunity. You're not going to rule the league at 19."

"Youngest player on the team," Fischer explained with a smile after being bumped from a dressing room stall to a folding chair near the refreshment table. "I'll just be waiting for my opportunity. You're not going to rule the league at 19." Fischer dressed for 52 games with the Wings, tallying eight assists and no goals. A frequent healthy scratch in Detroit, he spent a seven-game conditioning stint in January 2000 with Cincinnati of the American Hockey League. Yet at season's end the Detroit Sports Broadcasters Association voted Fischer the team's rookie of the year.

The 2000–01 campaign was much the same. Fischer won the Red Wings' 2000 Super Skills competition with a 100.5 mph slap shot but dressed for only 55 games (he missed eight with a sprained ankle). He spent five weeks in Cincinnati, returning to Detroit just before the March trade deadline. Shortly after, he finally scored his first NHL goal. It was March 17, 2001— St. Patrick's Day, appropriately—when Fischer banged a rebound past Colorado's Patrick Roy. That was the extent of his goal scoring that season.

Fischer got his first taste of NHL post-season action but the Red Wings were upset by Los Angeles in the first-round of the 2001 playoffs. The 2001–02 campaign would prove to be far more memorable. Fischer, by then beefed up to his current 225 pounds, lined up alongside veteran Chris Chelios for most of the season. Although his two goals and eight assists were not overly impressive, Fischer proved he belonged. Still the second youngest on the squad, he contributed three playoff goals and three assists towards the Wings' 2002 Stanley Cup victory. Fischer played every playoff game that spring, save one; the league office suspended Fischer for his stiff cross-check to the mouth of Carolina's Tommy Westlund. He missed the fifth and deciding game of the finals but quickly suited up to join the on-ice festivities and hoist the Cup.

On November 12, 2002, Fischer sustained a season-ending knee injury; surgery was required, but Fischer worked hard in anticipation of joining the Wings in the latter part of the playoffs. A first-round sweep by the Anaheim Mighty Ducks dashed that hope, but Fischer was more than ready for the 2003–04 campaign.

Red Wings coach Dave Lewis paired newly acquired tough guy Derian Hatcher—formerly the Dallas Stars captain—with Fischer in training camp. Fischer gave Hatcher the number 2 jersey he had worn to date and took number 8. Unfortunately, in only the third game of the season, Hatcher suffered the same knee injury that had crippled Fischer the previous season. Many asked if Fischer could make up for the loss of Hatcher's hitting.

"Every team needs players that will play hard, show strength in front of the net— and Derian was our leader," argued Fischer that night. "It's not going to be up to one player." But deeds speak louder than words. It was Fischer who crashed Vancouver Canuck Daniel Sedin through the Joe Louis Arena glass late in that game.

	GP	G	A	TP	PIM
RS	283	8	44	52	262
PO	38	4	3	7	55

AWARDS
Stanley Cup

DATE OF BIRTH
Trail, British Columbia
March 5, 1981–

NHL CAREER
2001–04
St. Louis

Barret Jackman

The St. Louis Blues invested time in a blue-chip prospect, and everyone profited. After selecting Barret Jackman with their first pick in the 1999 NHL entry draft, the feisty defenseman played two more seasons with his junior team in Regina. Jackman then spent the 2001–02 campaign with Worcester in the American Hockey League and made the AHL's All-Rookie Team. He joined the Blues for one regular-season contest and the final game of the 2002 Western Conference Finals, when St. Louis coach Joel Quenneville lauded him as the best player on the ice. At last, Jackman was ready for the big league, full time.

In 2002–03, Jackman took a regular spot in the Blues lineup. Quenneville, a former NHL defenseman himself, paired Jackman with savvy veteran Al MacInnis. The absence of star rearguard Chris Pronger due to a wrist injury left a huge hole on the St. Louis blue line. Jackman and MacInnis, a Norris Trophy finalist, filled it admirably. "This guy played like a 10-year veteran," praised MacInnis. "I'm not sure we would have finished where we did (99 points and fifth in their conference) if not for Barret. He was as consistent as any player on our team." Jackman's rugged style of play earned accolades around the rest of the league, too.

"This guy played like a 10-year veteran."

"Barret Jackman is the best rookie in the league by a substantial margin," said Calgary coach Darryl Sutter. "To play that position on a top offensive team that doesn't give up much the other way, to play as many minutes as he does and to have the respect that he does from everybody else in the league? To me, he is the hands-down rookie of the year." Jackson joined the 2003 NHL All-Rookie Team and, sure enough, won the coveted Calder Trophy as the NHL's top freshman.

"All credit goes to him and what he's kind of shaped me to be this year," said Jackman humbly of MacInnis. But Jackman, who led St. Louis with a plus-23 as a rookie, had much more going for him than MacInnis' mentorship. Unlike MacInnis, who perfectly fits the mold of the modern All-Star defenseman, Jackman is something of a throwback in style: a stay-at-home defenseman who doesn't rack up points yet still gets noticed. The first "defensive defenseman" ever to win the rookie award, Jackman also had the fewest points and the most penalty minutes of any Calder winner.

While a good skater, Jackman is not flashy. His shot is more than adequate, but nothing compared to MacInnis' howitzer. Jackman had three goals and 16 assists in 2002–03 versus MacInnis' sixteen and 52. MacInnis picked up 37 points on the power play; Jackman gathered none. MacInnis spent 61 minutes in the penalty box while Jackman tallied 190, second most on the Blues roster.

Many opponents were surprised at Jackson's toughness, but he'd proven himself back in junior. "He came in, fought all the tough guys and made his mark," said Regina Pats General Manager Brent Parker. "He's as tough a guy as we've had." Jackman accumulated 224 penalty minutes in his first year in junior and played for Team Canada in the World Under-17 Championships. The following season, at age 17, the Pats named him team captain; Jackman credits the extra responsibility with making him a better player.

Although Chris Pronger was back in the lineup for 2003–04, the defenseman's sophomore year might have been rockier. He'd lost the element of surprise that can give a rookie an edge. No matter; Jackman brings his own edge to the game. His play shows a mean streak, a quality All-Stars such as Chris Chelios and Derian Hatcher possess in spades and one that can't easily be nurtured if it's not innate. Off the ice, Jackman is friendly but reserved. On the ice, he's aggressive and belligerent, goading penalties by getting under an opponent's skin. While the referees might watch him more closely as a result, so too does the opposition. Jackman will continue to get the space and deference given to tough customers for many years to come.

	GP	G	A	TP	PIM	AWARDS
RS	98	4	18	22	231	Calder
PO	8	0	0	0	16	

Robyn Regehr

His hockey career was almost over before it began. In July 1999, Robyn Regehr was driving to his home in Rosthern, Saskatchewan, when an oncoming car swerved into his lane. The two men in the other car were killed, and Regehr went to hospital with a concussion and two badly broken legs. Many worried whether he would ever recover to play hockey.

"I always tried to stay positive," recalled Regehr two years later. "And when I was getting down in the dumps, my friends and my family kept me positive." Contrary to all predictions, Regehr stepped onto the ice for the Calgary Flames less than four months after the accident.

Originally drafted by the Colorado Avalanche in the first round of the 1998 NHL entry draft, Regehr was dealt to Calgary on February 28, 1999, while in the midst of his third season in junior with the Kamloops Blazers of the Western Hockey League. He made the WHL's 1999 First All-Star Team, concluding the season with 12 goals and 20 assists before leading his team to the league finals. The highly touted reaguard was expected to challenge for a spot on the Calgary roster, but with his near-fatal crash, all bets were off.

"When I was getting down in the dumps, my friends and my family kept me positive."

Regehr was back on skates in September, then made his professional debut in the minors with the American Hockey League's Saint John Flames in October. After a couple of weeks, he got the call to play for Calgary, and made a strong impression right from the start.

"He gets better all the time. He is going to be a real player in the NHL for a long time," said coach Brian Sutter. "This is a player who lost 10 pounds of muscle in the accident he hasn't regained. My goodness, he's fun to be around now and imagine how much better he could be with that much more strength." The six-foot-two teenager eventually bulked up to his current playing weight of 225.

A mid-season collision with teammate Jarome Iginla resulted in a concussion that cost him 11 games, but once again, Regehr showed resiliency. He finished his NHL rookie year with five goals and seven assists in 57 games and became the youngest nominee ever for the Bill Masterton Trophy, the league's award for perseverance and dedication to the game.

Brian Sutter was fired after the 1999–2000 season but new Flames coach Greg Gilbert was likewise impressed with Regehr. "He's made a real commitment to both himself and the team, just by the way he trains himself—he's a machine," said Gilbert.

Regehr stayed healthy for 71 games in his sophomore season and continued to receive kudos for his play. A slump in the 2001–02 campaign, however, had trade rumors swirling. Regehr finished the year at minus-24—the worst on a team that finished out of the playoffs for the sixth consecutive time—averaging just under 21 minutes of ice time per game. Flames general manager Craig Button was quick to argue that a 21-year-old defenseman out against the league's top forwards was bound to encounter difficulties. He was rewarded for his patience with Regehr the following season.

Regehr tallied 12 points in 2002–03—all assists—but patrolled the blue line with more intensity and a sharper edge. His inspired play improved even more mid-season when Duane Sutter—who likes an aggressive, even nasty, approach to the game—replaced Gilbert behind the bench.

"'Reg' is a big, strong guy," said Regehr's regular defense partner Toni Lydman. "He can put guys on the wall. I'm just collecting the change, just getting the loose pucks."

In the summer of 2003, Duane Sutter became general manager as well as coach. Calgary soon signed Regehr to a new five-year, $10.5-million contract. Sutter hailed him as a franchise cornerstone and Regehr looked forward to meeting those expectations.

"They want me to be a top defenseman on the team and I believe I can do that," he explained with enthusiasm. "I believe I can be a top defenseman in the *league*." At this point, few would disagree.

	GP	G	A	TP	PIM
RS	283	12	42	54	370
PO	26	2	7	9	20

The Goaltenders

The Goaltenders

"What pitching is in a short series in baseball," noted Detroit general manager Jack Adams, "goaltending is in the Stanley Cup playoffs." That such respect for the position comes from the man who traded Hall of Fame netminders Turk Broda, Alex Connell, Harry Lumley, Glenn Hall and, twice, Terry Sawchuk affirms what every fan of the game already knows: Tending goal is the most vulnerable position in hockey.

"How would you like it," Jacques Plante once asked rhetorically, "if every time you made a small mistake in your job, a red light went on over your desk and 15,000 people stood up and yelled at you?" While stories of other hockey players suffering nervous breakdowns are uncommon, they are legion about goaltenders.

"Goalies are insane," Glenn Hall once warned teenager Grant Fuhr, but the enthusiastic young student remained undeterred.

Perhaps Fuhr had heard Gump Worsley's take on the position: "Not all goaltenders are nuts; only about 90 percent of them."

What is surprising is how many of hockey's premier goalies first went between the pipes simply because they had no choice. At age 14, the four-foot-eleven Worsley was given an ultimatum. "You're going to have to forget about playing forward," his coach said, "and put on those goalie pads."

Said center Phil Esposito of his brother Tony, "He was younger, so he had to be the goalie."

While hockey has evolved over the years, nowhere have the changes been more dramatic than in goaltending. Until 1917, a goalie was penalized for dropping to his knees. Various restrictions on a goalie's ability to hold and freeze the puck were implemented in the first half of the twentieth century, and even the blocker and catcher—now seen as rudimentary tools of the trade—didn't become standard issue until the 1940s. In 1959, Jacques Plante literally changed the face of goaltending when he ushered in the era of the mask. Continual refinements have succeeded in making the position safer, but the tremendous increase in the size of the goaler's equipment coincident with fewer goals being scored has caused new rules to be written again, this time to limit its dimensions.

Because of such profound transformations, it is more difficult to draw comparisons between goalies of different eras than it is to compare, for instance, different generations of skaters. But what these goaltending legends do share are the skills and fortitude to adjust to the demands of goaltending as we now understand it.

Wisdom has it that a goalie's skills peak at about age 30. If so, then the younger netminders highlighted here still have their best hockey ahead of them. Goaltending has never been as strong as it is today—perhaps the by-product of better equipment, training and coaching. But since television highlight reels still concentrate on the pucks that go in more than the pucks the goalies turn away, the NHL is constantly challenged to tinker with the rules to increase scoring. Like their counterparts before them, though, these young goalies will continue to develop better ways to keep the puck out of the net.

LEGENDS

- Johnny Bower
- Frank Brimsek
- Turk Broda
- Ken Dryden
- Bill Durnan
- Grant Fuhr
- Glenn Hall
- Dominik Hasek
- Bernie Parent
- Jacques Plante
- Patrick Roy
- Terry Sawchuk
- Billy Smith
- Vladislav Tretiak
- Gump Worsley

YOUNG LIONS

- Dan Blackburn
- Rick DiPietro
- Mark-Andre Fleury
- Roberto Luongo
- Andrew Raycroft

Opposite: Innovative goaltending legend Jacques Plante was an NHL All-Star in three different decades. Previous page: Dominik Hasek won six Vezina Trophies with Buffalo before winning a Stanley Cup ring with Detroit in 2002.

Johnny Bower

It's difficult to picture Johnny Bower as a young man, much less a boy. His wizened face, unmasked until his final season, was almost as creased and laugh-lined when he entered the league at the age of 29 as it was when he retired at 45. Bower added hundreds more scars over the span of his career, but he accepted them as an occupational hazard. "I just made up my mind I was going to lose teeth and have my face cut to pieces," he said in explaining his decision to become a goalie. "It was easy."

Bower's real age was a subject of some debate, since he had lied about it in order to join the army during World War II. Amazingly, the four-year war veteran was still eligible to play junior hockey when he returned to civilian life. Bower spent a season back home in Prince Albert, Saskatchewan, then joined the Cleveland Barons in the American Hockey League in 1945.

The New York Rangers gave him his first shot at the big time in the 1953–54 season. Goaltender Chuck Rayner, who had just retired, gave the rookie goalie tips on his stick work, particularly the poke-check. It would become Bower's signature move.

"I wasn't all that glad to see the two-goalie system come in."

Acquitting himself admirably that season with New York, Bower played every minute of every game. He had five shutouts on a team that finished out of the playoffs, posting a 2.60 goals-against average. But the Rangers brought in goalie Gump Worsley and gave Bower a ticket back to the minors.

Bower spent the 1954–55 season with Vancouver in the Western Hockey League. A five-game call-up to the Rangers that year went well, but Bower was soon back to the AHL. He played only a couple of 1956–57 NHL games while racking up numerous AHL awards. Bower played brilliantly against the Springfield Indians in the 1958 playoffs. Fortuitously, the Indians were managed by Punch Imlach, soon to be installed as manager and coach of the Toronto Maple Leafs. That was just the break Bower needed.

Almost 34 years old when he was drafted by the Leafs in 1958, Bower initially shared duties with Ed Chadwick before establishing himself as Toronto's number-one—and only—goaltender for the next three years. He spent hours perfecting his poke-check. Jabbing his stick with his arm outstretched—often after making a spectacular dive to cover more distance and exercise the element of surprise—Bower could knock the puck off his opponent's stick so that his teammates could clear it out of harm's way. He won the Vezina Trophy and First All-Star Team honors in 1960–61.

As genial a player as any who has ever skated in the NHL, Bower was also extremely competitive. "I always played best under pressure," he said. "Maybe it was the money and prestige that went with the big games." With Bower, Toronto won three consecutive Stanley Cup victories in the early 1960s. The icing on the cake was the shutout he registered in Game Seven of the 1964 Stanley Cup finals. Opposite him in the Detroit Red Wings goal was the legendary Terry Sawchuk, who was traded to Toronto for the 1964–65 season.

Sawchuk and Bower made a potent team. They shared the Vezina Trophy in 1965, and their success prompted the NHL to institute a new rule requiring every club to dress two goalies for every game. "I wasn't all that glad to see the two-goalie system come in," maintained Bower. "I wanted to play in all the games I possibly could." But the two veterans tag-teamed to a surprising victory for Toronto in the 1967 Stanley Cup finals.

Bower retired after the 1968–69 campaign at age 44, although he was persuaded to suit up for one more game in the following season. At the summer goalie school he runs, students—prompted by parents and grandparents—still ask him to teach them the poke-check.

DATE OF BIRTH
Prince Albert, Saskatchewan
November 8, 1924–

NHL CAREER
1953–55, 1956–57, 1958–70, 1958–70
NY Rangers, Toronto

	GP	W	L	SO	AVE
RS	552	250	195	37	2.52
PO	74	35	34	5	2.54

AWARDS

1st All-Star, Vezina (2),
Stanley Cup (4), HOF 1976

149

Frank Brimsek

"Usually when the Bruins entered, there would be a lot of cheering," recalled goaltender Frank Brimsek, looking back at a game against the Montreal Canadiens on December 1, 1938. "But when I hit the ice, things were so quiet that I could hear the people breathing. They were just waiting for me to blow one."

Earlier in the season, Brimsek had made a quiet rookie debut in the Boston net as a temporary substitute for the legendary "Tiny" Thompson. After missing only two games due to an eye infection, Thompson returned, but Brimsek had obviously made a huge impression on Boston's management. A month later, Boston sold Thompson to Detroit.

Several players, including the levelheaded Dit Clapper, threatened to quit, convinced that they'd never win without Thompson. Not only was Brimsek American-born, his parents were Slovenian emigrants. How could he ever succeed?

"I should have taken a rest before coming back, but I needed the money."

Brimsek lost his first test against Montreal 2-0, and the fans were on him throughout. But Brimsek shut out his opponents in the next three games, posted another victory, then three more consecutive shutouts. "Kid Zero"—soon to become "Mr. Zero" for the remainder of his career—received standing ovations from the Bruin faithful for the rest of the season. Brimsek's 1.56 goals-against average earned him the Vezina and Calder trophies and he became the first rookie to make the First All-Star Team. He lowered his average to 1.50 in the playoffs to help Boston win the Stanley Cup for the first time in 10 years.

Brimsek anchored the league's best team in the following two years, and Boston won the Cup again in 1941. "He's as quick as a cat," said New York Rangers manager Lester Patrick. "And trying to get him to make the first move is like pushing over [the] Washington Monument."

Detroit goalie Johnny Mowers added, "He's got the best left hand in the business, and nobody plays the angles as well as he does."

Constantly looking for an "edge on the offense," Brimsek also played a sharp mental game. "I always tried to make the opposition player do what I wanted him to," he explained. "I always felt that the glove side was the strongest side for a goaltender. And I would make the shooter believe this too. In

that way, I would make most shooters fire the puck to my stick side, which is what I wanted them to do in the first place."

In 1943, Brimsek joined the U.S. Coast Guard. While he spent some time tending goal for the Coast Guard Clippers, he then endured 18 months of active duty in the South Pacific with a Coast Guard supply ship. The experience changed him profoundly. "I came back too soon after being in the service," admitted Brimsek. "My nerves were jumpy. I should have taken a rest before coming back, but I needed the money."

DATE OF BIRTH
Eveleth, Minnesota
September 26, 1915–November 11, 1998

NHL CAREER
1938-43, 1945-50
Boston, Chicago

He returned to the NHL midway through the 1945–46 season, but Brimsek's playing days were numbered. "When I got out of the war, I knew I wasn't going to play long. I didn't have that same feeling for the game," he said. "I had a hard time even going back to training camp." Yet Rocket Richard, who became a league star during Brimsek's military leave, called Brimsek "the toughest goalie I ever faced."

Brimsek made the Second All-Star Team three years in a row. Meanwhile, he was preparing for retirement. "I had spoken to [general manager] Art Ross in 1947 and told him that I would like to leave Boston in '49 to go to Chicago," said Brimsek. "My brother was starting a business there, and I thought I might help him open a few doors. Ross agreed, but when it came time, he

didn't like the idea anymore. 'If that's the way you feel,' I told him, 'I'll quit altogether!'"

Brimsek got his trade to Chicago, and even with the last-place Blackhawks, he added five more career shutouts in his final NHL season in 1950. In 1966, he became the first American elected to the Hockey Hall of Fame.

	GP	W	L	SO	AVE
RS	514	252	182	40	2.70
PO	68	32	36	2	2.56

AWARDS
1st All-Star (2), 2nd All-Star (6), Calder, Vezina (2), Stanley Cup (2), HOF 1966

Turk Broda

"He's the best playoff player in all hockey," claimed Toronto Maple Leafs owner and manager Conn Smythe, and when Turk Broda died in 1972, his record of 13 playoff shutouts still stood. "The bonus money for winning wasn't much," laughed the lighthearted Broda, "but I always needed it."

Walter Broda earned his nickname as a child, when his class was told the story of an old English king called "Turkey Egg" by his subjects because of his freckles. Since Broda had more freckles than any of his schoolmates, the moniker became his as well. Soon, it was just "Turk," and the tag stuck.

Broda turned professional with Detroit's International League farm club in 1935. "He hasn't a nerve in his body," declared Red Wings general manager Jack Adams. "He could play in a tornado and never blink an eye." But in 1936, Smythe acquired the promising netminder for $8,000.

"He could play in a tornado and never blink an eye."

After five strong seasons, Broda won his first Vezina Trophy in 1940–41. The following season, he backstopped his team in the most remarkable comeback in Stanley Cup history. Down three games to none, he allowed only seven goals in the next four games to help the Leafs to their first championship in 10 years.

By 1945, the next time Toronto won the Stanley Cup, Broda had been in the army for almost two years. A public controversy had erupted when the Royal Canadian Mounted Police stopped his train en route to Montreal, arrested Broda and returned him to Toronto—all so that he would play hockey for the Toronto Army Daggers rather than the Montreal military team, which had offered him a $2,400 bonus. The frustrated Broda would later complain that he had been drafted to stop pucks rather than bullets.

Broda returned to NHL duty late in the 1945–46 season. "We were outplayed and outchanced in scoring opportunities, I would think, by about three to two," said Toronto rookie Howie Meeker. "Turk Broda was the guy who won that series." The Leafs won their first of three consecutive Stanley Cups.

Broda's colorful character made him a crowd favorite. Before accepting his teammates' congratulations after a victory, he would rush around the ice scooping up the cigars his fans had showered down. His chubby face and portly build made him an unlikely-looking NHL star, and when the Leafs faltered, 35-year-old Broda was an easy target.

"If it isn't Turk's fault, we'll find out whose it is," said Smythe after the Leafs stumbled halfway through the 1949–50 season. "I'm taking Broda out of the nets, and he's not going back until he shows some common sense." To back up his threat that the five-foot nine-inch Broda wouldn't play until he shed seven of his 197 pounds, Smythe called up a reserve and then traded for up-and-coming netminder Al Rollins. "Two seasons ago, [Turk] weighed 185. Last season, he went up to 190—and now this," complained Smythe. "A goalie has to have fast reflexes, and you can't move fast when you're overweight."

Broda won the "Battle of the Bulge" by fasting and sweating his way down to the prescribed weight. He shed a further four pounds while earning a shutout in his first game back.

Although Broda played in 31 games, Rollins was awarded the Vezina Trophy for Toronto's 1950–51 season. But it was Broda who sparkled in eight of the Leafs' 11 playoff games. His minuscule 1.13 goals-against average helped Toronto to another Stanley Cup victory. That series, however, was Broda's swan song: He appeared in only three games the next year before retiring.

DATE OF BIRTH
Humboldt, Saskatchewan
May 15, 1914–October 17, 1972

NHL CAREER
1936-43, 1945-52
Toronto

	GP	W	L	SO	AVE
RS	629	302	224	62	2.53
PO	101	60	39	12	1.98

AWARDS
1st All-Star (2), 2nd All-Star, Vezina (2),
Stanley Cup (5), HOF 1967

Ken Dryden

In 1972, Ken Dryden took time out from sightseeing with Team Canada to visit the hockey department of the Institute of Physical Culture and Sport in Moscow. The Soviets' scientific approach led one official to insist that Dryden was too tall to be a goaltender. "There are disadvantages," the six-foot-four Dryden conceded, "but there are advantages too: my reach. I can cover a lot of goal." His host was unconvinced, but NHL shooters knew better. While he played fewer than eight NHL seasons, Dryden was goalie for six Stanley Cup winning teams, had six All-Star campaigns, and he never lost more than 10 games in any one campaign.

"The team always felt that [Dryden] could win them a big game if he had to," said coaching legend Scotty Bowman, whose career with the Habs began in Dryden's rookie year (1971–72) and ended with his netminder's retirement in 1979. "He was the most consistent goaltender I have ever coached, and a fierce competitor."

"The team always felt that he could win them a big game if he had to."

Dryden followed his brother Dave's lead. Their first meeting on NHL ice on March 2, 1971—with veteran Dave in net for the Buffalo Sabres and call-up Ken guarding Montreal's cage—replicated hundreds of backyard games. But the brothers had taken radically different routes to the NHL. Dryden spurned Canadian junior hockey to play four years at Cornell University while working toward a law degree, an unlikely path to the NHL in the 1960s. Although the Montreal Canadiens were interested in his services, Dryden accepted an offer with the Canadian national team that would allow him to continue his education.

When the national team program folded a year later, Dryden entered the Montreal farm system. It wasn't long before he was brought up to the parent club, and he played in the last six games of the 1970–71 season. He won every match and posted a 1.65 goals-against average, but the hockey world was stunned when Montreal started him against the defending Stanley Cup champion Boston Bruins in the first playoff game that spring.

The Bruins had finished 24 points ahead of the Habs that season. But Dryden backstopped the Canadiens to a seven-game upset and eventually won the Conn Smythe Trophy for his part in vanquishing Minnesota and Chicago en route to a Stanley Cup victory. He proved that it was more than beginner's luck when he won the Calder Trophy the next season, his official rookie year. He earned his second Stanley Cup ring in 1973, but

dissatisfied with his contract, Dryden shocked fans and pundits alike when he quit the game that year to return to his legal career.

When Montreal faltered badly without Dryden in the 1973–74 season, the club offered to quadruple his salary, raising it to the going rate for the NHL's best talent. The following season, Dryden once again traded his legal pads for goalie pads.

His "leave of absence" had just been part of hard bargaining, and he quickly picked up where he had left off. A year after his return, Dryden backstopped Montreal to four consecutive Stanley Cups.

Dryden's iconic pose—gloves stacked on the butt end of his stick, chin resting on his blocker—was original and unforgettable. While the image epitomized the thinker he was, it was also a ritual that helped him stretch out a long spine that spent too much time in a crouch. Unfortunately, Dryden's back finally got the better of him, and in 1979, he announced his retirement, this time for good.

His book *The Game*, arguably hockey's greatest tome, launched him into a successful writing and broadcasting career. In 1997, he moved into an executive position with the Toronto Maple Leafs, and in 2004, he was elected to the Canadian parliament.

DATE OF BIRTH
Hamilton, Ontario
August 8, 1947–

NHL CAREER
1971-73, 1974-79
Montreal

	GP	W	L	SO	AVE
RS	397	258	57	46	2.24
PO	112	80	32	10	2.40

AWARDS

1st All-Star (5), 2nd All-Star,
Vezina (5), Stanley Cup (6), HOF 1983

Bill Durnan

Bill Durnan tended goal with a unique pair of gloves—fingered catching mitts that allowed him to hold his goalie's stick in either hand, and to adjust his stance to face an attacker with a catching glove always in the optimum position, covering the wider part of the net. He credited Steve Faulkner, his boyhood coach, with his ambidextrous ability. "He worked me by the hour," explained Durnan, "until I had the technique down pat, and we won five city championships in six years. At first, it felt as though I was transferring a telephone pole from one hand to the other, but after a while, I'd hardly realize I was doing it." Not only ambidextrous, Durnan also had lightning reflexes, particularly in his hands, a combination that confounded shooters throughout his career.

"They booed me and made me feel six inches high."

Durnan was originally signed by the Toronto Maple Leafs in 1936. He won junior hockey's Memorial Cup while playing in the Leafs' farm system and was ready to go to his first NHL training camp. Unfortunately, just before camp opened, he injured his knee in a playful tussle with a friend. When the Leafs heard about his injury, they immediately dropped him from their protected list.

Durnan angrily vowed never to play in the NHL, even drifting from hockey for a time after his knee healed. Before long, though, he was active in the mercantile leagues, playing goal in the winter and baseball in the summer as a pitcher, always with a guaranteed company job to augment his income. He starred for several teams, including the Kirkland Lake Blue Devils, which won hockey's Allan Cup in 1940—a prestigious trophy at the time.

In 1940–41, Durnan began tending net for the Montreal Royals in the Quebec senior league. He was content, but in 1943, he started to feel considerable pressure to play for the Canadiens. "Somehow, I managed to hold out until the day of the opening game," he explained years after he finally gave in. "I signed for the huge sum of $4,200 and found myself on a hockey team just beginning to jell." Durnan won the Vezina Trophy and a First All-Star Team selection, as he would in five of the next six seasons.

Durnan and the rest of the Canadiens slumped badly in the 1947–48 season, and the Montreal fans voiced their displeasure.

"They booed me and made me feel six inches high," Durnan lamented. "I don't know whether you've ever heard 13,000 people all calling you the same bad name at the same time, but it sure makes a loud noise." Durnan threatened to quit, but was persuaded to stay and rebounded with two more excellent seasons.

Durnan looked back at the 1949–50 campaign as "the beginning of the end." He decided to quit at season's end. "I'll admit," he conceded in 1972, "if they were paying the kind of money goaltenders get today, they'd have had to shoot me to get me out of the game. But at the end of any given season, I never had more than $2,000 in the bank. I wasn't educated and had two little girls to raise. All this worried me a great deal, and I was also hurting."

Heavily favored Montreal faced New York in the first round of the 1950 playoffs, but the Rangers jumped into a 3-0 lead in games. Durnan decided that Gerry McNeil, a promising young goalie pegged as his eventual replacement, might as well start the next game.

While admitting that the emotional turmoil he felt was agonizing, "the nerves and all the accompanying crap," Durnan attested, "were built up." Yet the story went out that Durnan couldn't handle the pressure and had suffered a nervous breakdown. McNeil started game four and Durnan never played another hockey game.

DATE OF BIRTH
Toronto, Ontario
January 22, 1916–October 31, 1972

NHL CAREER
1943–50
Montreal

	GP	W	L	SO	AVE
RS	383	208	112	34	2.36
PO	45	27	18	2	2.07

AWARDS

1st All-Star (6), Vezina (6),
Stanley Cup (2), HOF 1964

Grant Fuhr

Grant Fuhr got off to an inauspicious start with the St. Louis Blues, showing up for training camp in 1995 almost 25 pounds overweight. The goalie was immediately sent packing by coach and general manager "Iron Mike" Keenan. A week later—and 14 pounds lighter—Fuhr returned. By the beginning of the season, he was down to his regular weight of 200 pounds and back in Keenan's good graces. Fuhr was in net for the first match of that campaign and went on to set an NHL record for goaltenders by starting 79 games in one season—76 in succession.

"He feels more comfortable in his hockey equipment than he does in his pajamas."

The move to St. Louis proved to be a tonic for Fuhr. Following 10 spectacular and glory-filled seasons with the Edmonton Oilers, Fuhr had been traded to the Toronto Maple Leafs in 1991 after publicly acknowledging a drug-abuse problem. He had a decent season with the Leafs, but Felix Potvin also arrived that year. Fuhr coached Potvin well enough that he was unseated as Toronto's "go-to" goaltender. Early in 1993, the Leafs sent Fuhr to the Buffalo Sabres. Unfortunately for Fuhr, Dominik Hasek was just emerging as a star. While the two shared the William M. Jennings Trophy with the league's lowest average in the 1993–94 season, Fuhr, as second-stringer, was dealt to the Los Angeles Kings only three games into the following season. There his average, never his strong suit, ballooned for the first time to more than four goals a game. In the summer of 1995, he arrived in St. Louis as a free agent.

After his initial blowup with Keenan, Fuhr, once again at his acrobatic best—with perhaps the league's sharpest reflexes—posted his lowest seasonal average.

"I've often learned things the hard way," said Fuhr, but for the longest time, everything had seemed to come easily to him. His 78-21-1 junior record had prompted Edmonton to use its first-round (eighth overall) draft pick in 1981 to choose him. Midway through his rookie NHL season, at the age of 19, Fuhr became the youngest goalie to play in an NHL All-Star Game. At season's end, he was runner-up in Vezina Trophy voting and selected for the Second All-Star Team. "He was born to be a goaltender," Mark Messier once said. "I'm sure he feels more comfortable in his hockey equipment than he does in his pajamas."

In Edmonton, a power struggle between goalies Fuhr and Andy Moog soon emerged. Both netminders shared regular-season duties, but Fuhr got almost all the calls in the playoffs. "Fuhr is one of the most unflappable athletes I have ever met," said ESPN broadcaster Darren Pang, a former NHL goaltender. "There is no pulse in the most pressurized situations, and that has always been his greatest asset." Fuhr backed the Oilers to four Stanley Cup victories in five years. While Edmonton's run-and-gun style meant that they gave up almost as many scoring opportunities as they created, Fuhr shone under the heavy workload. Although he didn't play the puck as much as many goalers, he nevertheless set an NHL record in 1983–84 for most points in a season, with 14 assists.

Fuhr used his star turn for Canada's winning team in the 1987 Canada Cup tournament as a springboard for his best NHL season. When Moog departed in frustration, Fuhr led the league in minutes played en route to his selection to the First All-Star Team and his only Vezina Trophy. He succumbed to his first serious injury two years later, and Bill Ranford stepped into the breach. Healed but on the bench, Fuhr watched his team win the Stanley Cup again in 1990.

During four seasons with the Blues, the injuries started to come more frequently. Fuhr was dealt to the Calgary Flames for the 1999–2000 campaign, but he never truly found his groove there. Fuhr announced his retirement at season's end. In 2003, he entered the Hall of Fame and the Edmonton Oilers retired his number 31.

DATE OF BIRTH
Spruce Grove, Alberta
September 28, 1962–

NHL CAREER
1981–2000
Edmonton, Toronto, Buffalo, Los Angeles, St Louis, Calgary

	GP	W	L	SO	AVE
RS	868	403	295	25	3.38
PO	150	92	50	6	2.92

AWARDS
1st All-Star, 2nd All-Star, Jennings,
Vezina, Stanley Cup (5), HOF 2003

Glenn Hall

Records are made to be broken, but goaltender Glenn Hall's record for consecutive games will never be bettered. From the first game of the 1955–56 campaign until 12 games into the 1962–63 season, Hall never missed a minute of NHL action. Finally, on November 7, 1962, Hall pulled himself out of a game against Boston due to back problems. When the Bruins scored on their first shot of the game, Hall went to the bench, conferred briefly with his coach then headed for the dressing room.

As Hall explained later, "I was able to take a comfortable stance, but I couldn't move with the play when it crossed in front of the net. A goalie who can't do that might as well be up in the stands." Hall's streak ended at 502 games—552 including playoffs. It remains one of the most remarkable accomplishments in hockey history.

On October 2, 1955, Hall played for the defending Stanley Cup champion Detroit Red Wings in his first of a record 13 All-Star Games (he had played just eight NHL games before that preseason game but showed such promise, the Red Wings traded away the great Terry Sawchuk). At season's end, Hall led the league in shutouts, a feat he repeated five times, and was voted rookie of the year.

"It was survival, number one."

Hall always spoke his mind, a trait that led Detroit general manager Jack Adams to trade him in 1957 to the sad-sack Chicago Blackhawks, along with Players' Association organizer Ted Lindsay. Hall, however, never missed a beat. Four years later, he backstopped the Blackhawks to the Stanley Cup.

Hall knew what worked for him and had the courage to stick with it despite the criticism he faced. He pioneered the "butterfly" style of goaltending, having discovered that by crouching and keeping his legs spread below the knees, he could cover more of the net and still keep his body upright, ready to spring back to his feet. Protected by better equipment, goalies now spend most of their time fending off attackers while down in the butterfly position. In Hall's day, a goalie who went down too often risked taking a shot in the face. "Back then, the goalkeepers always thought survival," Hall said years later. "The styles have changed so much since the mask came in. We tried to get our feet over in front of the puck and the head out of the way. It was survival, number one." Hall himself did not wear a mask until the final two seasons of his career.

Ironically, "Mr. Goalie," as he was called, appeared to hate hockey. He was sick to his stomach before every game and often between periods. "Five minutes before a game or between a period, I didn't hear what a coach was saying because I was in total preparation," recalled Hall. "All I would be thinking about was what I had to do. During a game, when someone got ready to shoot, I'd already looked at the shot in my mind. I tried to prepare myself for every option." Hall's vomit bucket became part of his legend.

In 1967, Blackhawks management deemed Hall expendable and left the 36-year-old unprotected in the league's first expansion draft. The St. Louis Blues quickly made him their first selection. Hall was so spectacular while his team was being swept out of the 1968 Stanley Cup finals by the Montreal Canadiens that he was awarded the Conn Smythe Trophy as best playoff performer. He won the Vezina Trophy for lowest goals-against average for a third time when he shared goaltending duties with the even older Jacques Plante in 1968–69, earning a First All-Star Team selection the same season.

Hall finally retired in 1971 at the age of 40. He had moved into third place among the all-time shutout leaders with 84, a position he has held ever since.

DATE OF BIRTH
Humboldt, Saskatchewan
October 3, 1931–

NHL CAREER
1955–71
Detroit, Chicago, St. Louis

	GP	W	L	SO	AVE	AWARDS
RS	906	407	326	84	2.51	Calder, 1st All-Star (7), 2nd All-Star (4),
PO	115	49	65	6	2.79	Vezina (3), Smythe, Stanley Cup, HOF 1975

Dominik Hasek

"I would say, without question," said Wayne Gretzky in 1998, "that Dominik Hasek has proven to be the best player in the world the last two years. Not only for what he did for the Buffalo Sabres and for the NHL but for what he did for his country in the Olympic Games." Hasek took the Czech Republic into the medal round of the 1998 Winter Olympics in Nagano, helping to eliminate an NHL star-studded American squad before facing the Canadian favorites.

Hasek was almost perfect. He nursed a 1-0 lead with dozens of brilliant saves before Canada's Trevor Linden found a chink in Hasek's armor with a minute left on the clock. Both Hasek and Canadian netminder Patrick Roy were flawless in an overtime period, but under Olympic rules, there was a shootout to decide the winner. It was the "most intense pressure of my life," said Hasek, but he blanked all five Canadians, while the Czechs managed to slip one by Roy.

"I just try to stop the puck... with my head, whatever it takes."

Facing Russia in the final game, Hasek posted a shutout in a tense 1-0 victory. He went home with a gold medal around his neck and an Olympic goals-against average of less than one. "Hasek to the castle!" was the cry that rang out in Prague's central square, as hundreds of thousands milled about in celebration.

The Chicago Blackhawks had drafted Hasek with the 199th pick in the 1983 NHL entry draft, but despite lucrative Blackhawk contract offers, Hasek had no interest in coming to North America then. He was the Czech goaltender of the year from 1986–90 before joining Chicago's minor-league affiliate in Indianapolis in the 1990–91 season. He appeared in five games with the Blackhawks before splitting the following season between Chicago and Indianapolis. He compiled a 10-4-1 record with the Blackhawks, and was named to the 1992 NHL All-Rookie Team, but teammate Eddie Belfour was clearly number one. A trade to the Buffalo Sabres in August 1992 convinced Hasek not to head for home, and within a year, "The Dominator" established himself as the league's premier goaltender.

Hasek won the Vezina Trophy in his second season as a Sabre and five times after that. His 1.95 goals-against average in 1993–94 marked the first time a goalie had dropped below 2.00 in 20 years. The Hart Trophy, which had not gone to a goaltender since 1962, went to Hasek in both 1997 and 1998, along with the Pearson Award.

"He's got an advantage on a lot of shooters because of the reputation he's built up," observed Mats Sundin of the Toronto Maple Leafs. "Guys see him in the net and think they have to try something special to score a goal."

Hasek is unconvinced. "I always believe only in my hard work and my skills," he has commented. "I look at the stick. I look at the players, and I just try to stop the puck, try to win the game—stop the puck with my head,

DATE OF BIRTH
Pardubice, Czechoslovakia
January 29, 1965–

NHL CAREER
1990–2002, 2003–04
Chicago, Buffalo, Detroit, Ottawa

whatever it takes."

"He's done some things nobody's seen before," noted Buffalo coach Lindy Ruff, "dropping his stick and using his other hand, making saves with his head, rolling over and laying his arm on the ice, rolling over and kicking his legs up. He never says 'never' on any play." Hasek took the Sabres to the 1999 Stanley Cup finals, but requested a trade to a contender for 2001–02.

Hasek's new team, the Detroit Red Wings, finished high atop the league standings, and after Hasek helped the cause with six playoff shutouts, he drank from the Stanley Cup. He confirmed his immediate retirement plans several months later.

But after a year off, Hasek found that he missed the game. The Wings didn't hesitate to bring Hasek back, but plagued by a nagging groin injury, Hasek missed most of the 2003-04 campaign. He has joined Ottawa as a free agent.

	GP	W	L	SO	AVE
RS	595	296	192	63	2.23
PO	97	53	39	12	2.03

AWARDS
1st All-Star (6), Hart (2), Pearson (2), Jennings (2), Vezina (6), Stanley Cup

Bernie Parent

"The mask gives you protection, saves you a few hundred stitches," noted Bernie Parent, "but the best thing it does is hide your face from the crowd." Fame rather than shame was Parent's desire for concealing his features—the slogan "Only the Lord Saves More Than Bernie Parent" appeared frequently on signs at games and on bumper stickers all over Philadelphia.

Signed by the Boston Bruins when he was a teenager, Parent got his first big break in Junior A hockey playing for coach Hap Emms in Niagara Falls. "Until I turned 18, I didn't know what a goaltender was supposed to do," he has said. "I just did things by instinct." Emms taught him how to play the angles, and Parent made an auspicious NHL debut in 1965 when both of Boston's starting goalies were injured. "Parent has given this club the lift it needs," said Bruins coach Milt Schmidt. "He has all the moves, he stays up, and he stays remarkably cool."

"Plante was like a god to me. Now I was on the same team with him."

Although Parent completed a decent rookie year, his play slipped in his second season. "If an athlete ever tells you booing doesn't bother him," said Parent, "he's either in a trance or just plain ignorant." Parent was sent to the minors, and the Philadelphia Flyers made him their first pick in the expansion draft the following summer. He shared duties with Doug Favell for three seasons before being sent to the Toronto Maple Leafs midway through the 1970–71 season.

Though he was initially upset, Parent realized that the trade was fortunate when Jacques Plante shook his hand in the dressing room. "Plante was like a god to me," he later recalled. "Now I was on the same team with him."

"We'll be playing together," said Plante warmly, "so just ask if there is anything I can help you with." Parent discovered that his idol literally had a book on every shooter in the league and wrote notes on every arena regarding the play of the boards and even the lighting. By the end of the 1971–72 season, Parent had made Plante's scientific goaltending system his own.

The Miami Screaming Eagles of the fledgling World Hockey Association enticed Parent to jump to the new league in 1972. Miami folded its team before playing a game, and Parent's contract was picked up by the WHA's Philadelphia Blazers. He was ecstatic about returning to Philadelphia, and the heavy barrage of shots he faced in 65 games for the Blazers was just what he needed after Plante's tutoring. But one season in the WHA was enough. The club folded, and Parent managed to force Toronto to trade his NHL rights to the Philadelphia Flyers for the 1973–74 season.

"My first game [exhibition] back with the Flyers was a forgettable one," Parent laughingly recalled. "After 12 minutes, I had let in seven goals." But he notched four shutouts in his first 10 games of the regular season. Parent shared the Vezina Trophy with Chicago's Tony Esposito, and his stingy 2.02 goals-against average in the ensuing playoffs helped the Flyers march to the Stanley Cup final and defeat the favored Boston Bruins. Parent's stellar performance—punctuated with a 1-0 shutout in the clinching game—earned him the Conn Smythe Trophy.

"We know the exhilarating feeling only a player on a Stanley Cup winner can appreciate," he exclaimed after another MVP performance, when the Flyers won their second consecutive Cup. "It won't be easy for any team to take the Cup away." But Montreal swept them in the 1976 finals, and Parent never got that close again.

"Once a game starts, I forget about the shots and getting hurt," he said, but Parent was struck down midway through the 1978–79 season. A stick glanced up in a goalmouth scramble and jabbed him in the eye. A sympathetic reaction in the other eye left the goaltender in complete darkness for two weeks.

Fortunately, Parent's sight returned, but his playing career was over. His jersey was officially retired, and he turned his attention to sharing his wisdom with new generations of Philadelphia goalies.

DATE OF BIRTH
Montreal, Quebec
April 3, 1945–

NHL CAREER
1965–72, 1973–79
Boston, Philadelphia, Toronto

	GP	W	L	SO	AVE
RS	608	271	198	55	2.55
PO	71	38	33	6	2.43

AWARDS
1st All-Star (2), Vezina (2), Smythe (2),
Stanley Cup (2), HOF 1984

Jacques Plante

If Jacques Plante had not stood up to Montreal Canadiens coach Toe Blake on the night of November 2, 1959, the number of career-ending injuries suffered by the sport's goaltenders would have been far higher by now. When sniper Andy Bathgate of the New York Rangers ripped open Plante's nose with a backhand, Plante informed Blake that the only way he would go back in the nets that night was with his mask on, the one he had worn in practice for years.

With no backup goalie dressed and his team enjoying a 4-1 lead, Blake relented. Plante was allowed to wear the mask until his nose healed. The Canadiens promptly won their next 11 games with a masked man in net. Still, Blake made Plante stick to their agreement, and a healed and bare-faced Plante started the next game. The team lost, and Blake let Plante decide whether the mask had helped or hindered his play. Plante's mask went on for good, and the face of goaltending was forever changed.

"I would have been dead. No question."

Ten years later, Plante was able to argue that the mask had saved his life. The 41-year-old Plante was playing excellent goal for the St. Louis Blues in the 1970 Stanley Cup finals when a rising puck caught Plante just above the left eye, putting him out of the series with a concussion but no cut or fracture. Without the mask, said Plante, "I would have been dead. No question."

Plante was as eccentric as he was brilliant in the nets. He found knitting relaxing and made the tuques he liked to wear in net (he claimed they spared him a chill). Denied this comfort by Blake, who didn't like the look of it, Plante knit undershirts instead. An asthmatic, he often complained about breathing problems in certain locations and occasionally stayed in a different hotel from that of his teammates. This further distanced him from those who saw camaraderie as integral to success.

Plante was a private man off the ice and egotistical to boot, but on the ice, he was the ultimate team player. He constantly called out helpful advice to his teammates and was the first goalie to signal impending icing calls for his defensemen. But Plante's greatest contribution to the art of goaltending was his willingness to roam from the crease, a strategy that he first devised when he was playing in the Quebec junior league during its expansion from 4 to 11 teams in 1947. "They needed all the players they could get," he explained. "We had four defensemen. One couldn't skate backwards. One couldn't turn to his left. The others were slow. It was a case of me having to go and get the puck when it was shot into our end because our defense couldn't get there fast enough. The more I did it, the farther I went. It seemed to be the best thing to do, so I did it, and it worked."

Despite his success with the powerhouse Canadiens of the 1950s, Plante eventually wore out his welcome in Montreal. The Canadiens faltered three times after five consecutive Stanley Cups, and in 1963, Plante was sent to the Rangers in a trade for Gump Worsley. Plante bragged that he'd win his seventh Vezina Trophy in New York, but playing for such a weak club seemed to cause him to lose heart. Suffering a demotion to the minors, he retired, demoralized, in 1965.

In 1968, however, the St. Louis Blues lured him back to share goaltending duties with Glenn Hall, and the two veterans shared the Vezina Trophy in 1968–69. The rejuvenated Plante played well into his forties. Sold to Toronto in 1970, he was dealt to Boston near the end of the 1972–73 campaign, his last in the NHL. Plant had one final stint with Edmonton in the WHA in 1974–75 before retiring for good. He succumbed to cancer in 1986.

DATE OF BIRTH
Mount Carmel, Quebec
January 17, 1929–February 26, 1986

NHL CAREER
1952–65, 1968–73
Montreal, NY Rangers, St. Louis, Toronto, Boston

	GP	W	L	SO	AVE
RS	837	437	246	82	2.38
PO	112	71	36	15	2.17

AWARDS
All-Star (3), 2nd All-Star (4), Hart,
Vezina (7), Stanley Cup (6), HOF 1978

Patrick Roy

Nine goals against in half a game is a goaltender's nightmare, but that ordeal was one of the defining moments of Patrick Roy's career. On December 2, 1995, the powerhouse Detroit Red Wings sent a relentless barrage of shots at Roy as the Montreal Canadiens put in a particularly hapless effort. Mario Tremblay, Montreal's rookie coach, let Roy twist in the wind in front of a mocking Montreal Forum crowd for far too long. The score was 9-1 before Tremblay gave Roy a merciful hook.

Humiliated and enraged, Roy stormed over to Canadiens president Ronald Corey and vehemently declared that he'd played his last game for Montreal. Despite the circumstances, such a public display of insubordination made a trade inevitable. Four days later, Roy was dealt to Colorado.

When the Avalanche faced the Canadiens a few weeks later, Roy was at his best, stopping 37 of 39 shots, for a 5-2 victory. He added a final insult by flipping the puck at Tremblay when the game ended. "It made me feel so good. It was a mistake, but I don't regret it," Roy told the media after the game. "I'm an emotional person. I know sometimes it gets me in trouble, but I know it sometimes helps me to play better too."

"No more rats."

The Canadiens were eliminated in the first playoff round that season, but Roy backstopped his team to the Stanley Cup finals. The Avalanche won the first two games against the Florida Panthers—Roy let in only a single goal in each game. The Panthers potted two quick goals early in the third game, however, and Roy suffered a barrage of plastic rats from the Florida fans with each goal.

Unlike other goalies who had faced a similar rain of rodents that season, Roy refused to creep back into his net for protection. He skated in small circles, with the dignity of a zoo tiger having marshmallows tossed at him. As the rats were being scooped up by the maintenance crew, Roy skated over to the Colorado bench. "No more rats," he quietly told his teammates. He did not let in another goal in the series, helping Colorado complete a sweep with a triple overtime shutout in game four.

Overtime hockey was nothing new to Roy, who was in goal for the Montreal Canadiens' record-breaking run of 10 consecutive overtime wins in their 1993 Stanley Cup triumph. Those playoff victories cemented his reputation as one of the greatest pressure goalies of all time. Roy was awarded the Conn Smythe Trophy for the second time. It was a feat he had first accomplished as a 20-year-old rookie in 1985, the youngest winner ever. "I haven't seen goaltending like that in 14 years," said Larry Robinson at the time, alluding to Ken Dryden's amazing debut. Roy won a record third Smythe after the Avalanche's 2002 Cup victory.

Roy's use of visualization, initially reported as "talking to his goalposts," was a celebrated aspect of his game. While his confidence bordered on arrogance, it was as much a calculated technique as a personality trait. "A goalie has to show he's confident, to his teammates as well as himself," he explained. "You are the last guy before that special red line. You make yourself confident. You make yourself hard to beat."

Roy's style evolved from stand-up to butterfly, best suited to getting his large frame in the way of pucks he couldn't even see. His manner of going down to cover the bottom half of the net had long become standard practice among young goalies before Roy decided to retire, at the end of the 2002–03 season, while still at the top of his profession. He left holding the NHL career goaltending records for most games and most wins in both the regular season and the playoffs. The Avalanche retired his number in 2003.

DATE OF BIRTH
Quebec City, Quebec
October 5, 1965–

NHL CAREER
1985–2003
Montreal, Colorado

	GP	W	L	SO	AVE
RS	1029	551	315	66	2.54
PO	247	151	94	23	2.30

AWARDS
1st All-Star (4), 2nd All-Star (2), Vezina (3),
Jennings (5), Smythe (3), Stanley Cup (4)

Terry Sawchuk

Terry Sawchuk's triumphs as a goaltender serve as a counterpoint to his life off the ice. Even his boyhood success was tinged by sadness. His brother died of a heart attack at the age of 17, and 10-year-old Terry inherited his goalie equipment. "The pads were always around the house," Sawchuk explained, "and I fell into them." He was such a natural that he was playing junior hockey within five years and signed his first pro contract with Omaha, in the Detroit Red Wings organization, a few years later.

In 1950–51, Sawchuk played all 70 games and had 11 shutouts for the defending Stanley Cup champions in Detroit. He won the Calder Trophy and First All-Star Team honors. The next season, he earned a dozen shutouts and won the Vezina Trophy. But he saved the best for last: Detroit swept both 1952 playoff series, and Sawchuk let in only five goals over the eight games for a 0.63 goals-against average.

"We are the people who make health insurance popular."

Sawchuk got his name on the Stanley Cup again in 1954 and 1955. "We could always count on him to come up with the big save," recalled Hall of Fame defenseman Bob Goldham. "When I look back on those Stanley Cup series, what I remember is 'Ukey' making one big save after another. He was the greatest goaltender who ever lived."

"I try to concentrate on the puck," said Sawchuk, in trying to describe his style. "I'm not a holler guy. I have a very low crouching style; my reflexes are that way, I guess. I can see better through the legs than over some tall guy's shoulder." His vulnerability in placing his face so close to the action wasn't lost on him. "I'm scared every time they get near me," he admitted, and the injuries he sustained over the years—ranging from facial gouges to bone fractures and ruptured spinal disks—are almost incredible. He once quipped: "We are the people who make health insurance popular."

But Sawchuk was loath to miss a game, not wanting anyone else to have a chance to shine. His first NHL break came when he was called up to fill in for Detroit's injured goaltender Harry Lumley. Sawchuk sparkled over a seven-game stint, earning his first of a record 103 career shutouts, and Lumley was traded. After Glenn Hall filled in for Sawchuk for two games in the 1954–55 season, Sawchuk was deemed expendable and traded to the Boston Bruins.

Sawchuk had battled a weight problem over the years, tipping the scales at a portly 230 pounds in 1951 before eventually dropping to a gaunt 170 pounds. His fluttery nerves were typical of those in his profession, but the move to Boston only added to his problems. He quit the game briefly after suffering a nervous collapse. It took a trade back to Detroit in 1957 to get him on track again.

Sawchuk earned All-Star honors twice more in Detroit before the Toronto Maple Leafs picked him up in June 1964. He shared duties with Johnny Bower for three seasons, culminating in Toronto's 1967 upset victories over Chicago and Montreal to win the Stanley Cup. "I'd like to leave hockey like that," said Sawchuk, after an especially outstanding effort against the Blackhawks. "In good style."

It did not happen. "As soon as I go into the net, I bend down and take a sideways peek at the goalposts," Sawchuk once said. "If they look close, I know I'm going to have a good night. Some nights, those damn posts look a mile away." Sawchuk struggled in 1967–68 with Los Angeles, had a disappointing season with Detroit and spent his final year in the NHL being used sparingly by the New York Rangers. But a calamity followed. After engaging in a postseason tussle with a teammate, Sawchuk died in hospital of internal injuries. His induction into the Hockey Hall of Fame in 1971 marked the postscript to a brilliant but tragic career.

DATE OF BIRTH
Winnipeg, Manitoba
December 28, 1929–May 31, 1970

NHL CAREER
1950–70
Detroit, Boston, Toronto, Los Angeles, NY Rangers

	GP	W	L	SO	AVE	AWARDS
RS	971	447	330	103	2.52	1st All-Star (3), 2nd All-Star (4),
PO	104	54	48	12	2.54	Calder, Vezina (4), Stanley Cup (4), HOF 1971

Billy Smith

"I will match them insult for insult," Billy Smith once said, after giving the finger to New York Rangers' fans. One of hockey's greatest playoff goalies, "Battlin' Billy" provoked his opponents and their supporters alike. A fierce competitor, he was sometimes known to skip the traditional handshake after losing a playoff series.

"I never saw a goalie so willing to crack people across the ankles with his stick," said Gump Worsley in 1975.

Smith later admitted that he was overly preoccupied with keeping his crease clear of enemy forwards, but at the time, rules to protect the goaltender were less stringent than they are today and the crease was considerably smaller. "I don't bother people unless they're bothering me," he maintained in 1982. "I just try to give myself a little working room. But if a guy bothers me, then I retaliate." But in 1986, he stepped over the line. After breaking the jaw and cheekbone of Chicago's Curt Fraser, he sat out a six-game suspension.

"If a guy bothers me, then I retaliate."

Drafted by Los Angeles in 1970, Smith got only a five-game tryout with the Kings in 1971–72. His future brightened considerably when he was picked up in the 1972 expansion draft by the New York Islanders. They needed all the help they could get.

Despite playing for a last-place club, Smith showed confidence. Glenn "Chico" Resch became his netminding partner in 1974–75, and the two soon formed one of the NHL's strongest duos. Nervous about extending himself and getting injured, Smith was content to watch about half of the games from the bench. For the same reason, he avoided on-ice practice as much as possible, concentrating on tennis to enhance his footwork and pioneering the use of computer games and simulations in training to improve his hand-eye coordination.

Smith became the first NHL goalie to score a goal when he made a save against the Colorado Rockies in 1979. With the goaltender pulled during a delayed penalty call, Colorado defenseman Rob Ramage sent an errant pass back to the blue line, only to see it slide all the way into his own net. Smith, the last Islander to have touched the puck, was credited with the goal.

Only once did Smith post a better regular-season average than Resch. "But when it came to the playoffs," said Smith, "I always seemed to get on a roll. There was more pressure, which helped my concentration, and the game seemed a little easier." After several promising seasons, the Islanders won the Stanley Cup four consecutive years starting in 1980, with Smith in the cage for 20 of the 21 playoff games.

"They call [baseball slugger] Reggie Jackson Mr. October," noted Islanders coach Al Arbour. "'Smitty' is our Mr. April and Mr. May."

Smith's strong play eventually made Resch expendable. With rookie Roland Melanson as his partner in 1981–82, Smith had his best season. He was selected to the First All-Star Team and received the Vezina Trophy, the first time the NHL's general managers voted for the league's best goalie.

Many wondered whether the three-year Islanders' dynasty would crumble before the Edmonton Oilers' offensive juggernaut in the 1983 Stanley Cup finals. Not only did Smith meet the Oilers with "probably the finest game I ever played," shutting them out 2-0 in the series opener, but he also denied Wayne Gretzky a single goal in a four-game sweep. Smith was awarded the Conn Smythe Trophy.

The Oilers succeeded in knocking the Islanders off in the next season's final series, and Smith's team went into a rebuilding phase. By then the last of the original Islanders, Smith continued to play well until his retirement in 1989. The Islanders retired his jersey number 31 in 1993, the year Smith was inducted into the Hockey Hall of Fame.

DATE OF BIRTH
Perth, Ontario
December 12, 1950–

NHL CAREER
1971–89
Los Angeles, NY Islanders

	GP	W	L	SO	AVE	AWARDS
RS	680	305	233	22	3.17	1st All-Star, Jennings, Vezina, Smythe,
PO	132	88	36	5	2.73	Stanley Cup (4), HOF 1993

Vladislav Tretiak

NHL hockey fans, especially in Canada, waited with glee for the beginning of the 1972 Summit Series. Canada's professionals would finally prove their vast superiority over the Soviet Union, which had been dominating international hockey for a generation with its "amateurs."

While preparing for the first game in Canada, 20-year-old Soviet goaltender Vladislav Tretiak received a surprise visitor, who brought along his own translator. "He meticulously told me, as a goalie, how to play the big Canadian shooters," recalled Tretiak. "Then he shook my hand and left. I can't explain why he came to give me secrets against his own players. Maybe he felt pity that I was so inexperienced, pity for a boy he thought Phil Esposito was going to tear apart. I wish to thank Jacques Plante for his advice."

Team Canada's scouts had reported that Tretiak was the weakest part of his team, but the opposite was true. The Canadian goalies detected Plante's influence right away, but the acrobatic Tretiak brought more than insider information to the game. "If there is a comparison to an NHL goalie I would make for Tretiak," remarked Paul Henderson, whose last-minute heroics in the final game gave Canada the narrowest of victories, "it would be Terry Sawchuk."

"I would have loved to play in Montreal."

Over the course of his career, Tretiak won 10 World Championship gold medals, three Olympic golds and one Olympic silver. He was on a record 13 Soviet League Championship teams, selected Soviet Player of the Year five times and was winner of the Gold Stick three times as the season's outstanding European player. These are tremendous achievements, but it was his play against the NHL pros that elevated him to mythic status in North America.

Many still remember the game played in the Montreal Forum on New Year's Eve 1976. Tretiak's Red Army went head-to-head against the Montreal Canadiens' dynastic club, backstopped by Ken Dryden. Outshot 38-13, the Soviets earned a 3-3 draw due almost solely to Tretiak's superb play. He was in net when the Soviets beat the NHL All-Stars in the 1979 Challenge Cup, a three-game tournament in Madison Square Garden. In the 1981 Canada Cup tournament, he led his team to victory, allowing only eight goals in six games. "He had better concentration," remarked Wayne Gretzky, "than any goalie I've ever seen."

After picking up clues that Tretiak might be interested in joining them, the Montreal Canadiens selected him in the 1983 NHL entry draft. The Soviet Ice Hockey Federation forbade Tretiak to leave. And in the Soviet era, it was not even possible for Tretiak to acknowledge that he had asked for permission. "I would have loved to play in Montreal," he admitted in later years, but the dissolution of the Soviet Union came too late for him.

After 15 seasons of playing almost every game for the national team and his own club, Tretiak was burned out. "I reached a point where I got tired of the hockey uniform," he admitted, "and didn't want to put it on anymore." In 1972, he had been given Jacques Plante's book on goaltending. "It seemed to me at that time that he spent too much time on the psychological strains experienced by goalies," said Tretiak. "Now I know how right he was."

Tretiak retired in 1984 and eventually took a job as goaltender coach for the Chicago Blackhawks, a position he still holds. In the 1999 Stanley Cup finals, the two opposing goalies were former students: Buffalo's Dominik Hasek and Dallas' Ed Belfour. Belfour, now with Toronto, still wears number 20 in tribute to Tretiak.

DATE OF BIRTH
Dmitrovo, Russia
April 25, 1952–

NHL CAREER
No NHL experience

AWARDS
HOF 1989

Lorne "Gump" Worsley

"If you want to be a good goaltender," claimed Gump Worsley, "it helps to be a little crazy."

Worsley had a wry wit, and his round face and pudgy physique added another dimension to his comic persona. A boyhood friend in Montreal had named him after the comic-strip character Andy Gump, and Worsley was so short that for his own safety, he wasn't allowed to play any position but goal. But there was nothing funny about Worsley's work in net.

"Chuck Rayner taught me how to cut down the shooters' angles and how to position myself in the net on breakaways," said Worsley, describing the help that soon-to-retire veteran goalie Chuck Rayner gave him in his 1952–53 rookie year with the New York Rangers. "Hell, he taught me everything he knew—and that was a lot. Without his guidance and encouragement, I'd probably never have made the grade."

"Nothing has ever matched that thrill."

Despite playing for a last-place club, Worsley won the Calder Trophy, but the Rangers responded to his request for a raise by bringing in Johnny Bower to replace him. Worsley spent a season back in the minors, but he replaced Bower in turn the following year.

The Rangers fluctuated between NHL mediocrity and inferiority, and Worsley later admitted that he sometimes used the bottle "to chase all those bad games and bad goals away." But he retained his sense of humor. His response to a reporter's question of which team gave him the most trouble—"The Rangers"—remains one of hockey's best quips. While facing a barrage of shots every night—50 to 60 was not uncommon—Worsley posted a decent goals-against average of 3.10 over 10 seasons with New York. He saw his trade to Montreal in the summer of 1963 as a chance to "get out of the Rangers jailhouse," but Worsley had difficulty establishing his place in Montreal. In his eighth game with the Habs, he pulled a hamstring muscle. A week later, he was sent to the minors to get in shape, and he didn't make it back until almost a year and a half later.

Facing the possibility that his NHL career was over, Worsley worked hard to reestablish himself as Montreal's number-one netminder. "The Gumper" tasted his first Stanley Cup champagne in the spring of 1965. "Nothing has ever matched that thrill," he said. Voted Second All-Star Team goaltender, Worsley shared the Vezina Trophy with Charlie Hodge and won the Cup again the following season.

Worsley played what was arguably his best hockey during the 1967–68 season. He shared the Vezina Trophy with Rogie Vachon and took First All-Star Team honors, and Montreal won the Cup again. His only frustration was seeing St. Louis netminder Glenn Hall awarded the Conn Smythe Trophy. While he liked and admired Hall—the two had swapped "trade secrets" about shooters on other teams over the years—Worsley had helped take his team to the Stanley Cup only to see the other goaltender receive the award for most valuable playoff performer for a second time. Detroit's Roger Crozier had won it in 1966.

"The abuse we goaltenders are forced to accept sometimes becomes intolerable," said Worsley. "That's why so many of us suffer nervous breakdowns." Claude Ruel—Montreal's new coach—didn't allow his aging goalie the latitude in practice that Toe Blake had permitted, and the frequent air travel due to league expansion was wearing on Worsley, who was a white-knuckle flyer. He suffered an emotional collapse during the season but came back and helped Montreal to another championship in 1969, his fourth. Early in the next season, Worsley was sent to the minors. He went home instead.

Wren Blair of the Minnesota North Stars persuaded him to play the rest of the season for him, and Worsley stayed for five years. He let his brush-cut hair grow longer and had another rebirth at the age of 42. Only Chicago goalie Tony Esposito finished with a lower average in the 1971–72 season. Worsley retired in 1974, shortly before turning 45.

DATE OF BIRTH
Montreal, Quebec
May 14, 1929–

NHL CAREER
1952–53, 1954–74
New York, Montreal, Minnesota

	GP	W	L	SO	AVE
RS	862	335	352	43	2.90
PO	70	88	36	5	2.82

AWARDS

Calder, 1st All-Star, 2nd All-Star, Vezina (2),
Stanley Cup (4), HOF 1980

DATE OF BIRTH
Montreal, Quebec
May 20, 1983–

NHL CAREER
2001–03
NY Rangers

Dan Blackburn

"He's not a loner. He's quiet and grounded," said Rangers broadcaster John Davidson. A teenaged goaltending prodigy himself back in the 1970s, Davidson knew firsthand the pressures an Albertan boy would face when thrown into the NHL spotlight. After the New York Rangers selected Dan Blackburn with the tenth overall draft pick in 2001, Davidson invited the young netminder to live with him and his family. Blackburn stayed for more than a year.

Back in 1999–2000, Blackburn first garnered national attention as a 16-year-old standout with the Kootenay Ice. He took the Western Hockey League by storm, posting 34 wins, 8 losses and 7 ties, and backstopped the Ice all the way to the Memorial Cup finals. He added the league's playoff MVP title to his growing list of awards, including WHL and Canadian Major Junior Rookie of the Year. The following season, he made the Canadian Major Junior First All-Star Team and was Goaltender of the Year.

Blackburn had developed a hybrid style—part stand-up, part butterfly—and a mental toughness that belied his young age. With quick reflexes, good concentration and effective positioning, he had the tools to be effective in the NHL; instead of returning to junior hockey, 18-year-old Blackburn went to "the show" in New York.

"When you need a break, it's usually just a mental break."

For most of the 2001–02 season, Blackburn served as veteran Mike Richter's understudy. He earned his first NHL victory on October 15, a 2-1 win in Montreal, becoming the third youngest game-winning goalie in NHL history. Blackburn played the last 9 games of the year while Richter nursed a head injury, for a total of 31 NHL appearances over the season. His 3.28 goals-against average and .898 save percentage earned Blackburn a spot on the NHL's 2002 All-Rookie Team.

By the opening of the 2002–03 campaign, Richter had re-signed with New York as a free agent. "I really wanted him back," said Blackburn with relief. "We've become really close and I knew it would help me, having him around." He also liked that Richter no longer got 65–70 starts a season. "Mike doesn't play as much as some other star goalies do," said Blackburn. "If someone like Curtis Joseph came, I wouldn't be on the ice as much as I was last year."

Blackburn soon got even more ice time than he expected. Barely over a month into the schedule, Richter went down with a concussion, and all goaltending responsibilities fell onto Blackburn's shoulders. He performed strongly, even notching his first NHL shutout—a 1-0 overtime win over Calgary—in the first game Richter missed.

"In junior, I used to play 20, 25 games in a row without thinking about it. It's not a big deal," Blackburn said, dismissing concerns he couldn't handle the workload. "I think I'll be fine for a while. When you need a break, it's usually just a mental break. . . . I want to take as much advantage of the situation as possible."

Yet, over 17 consecutive starts, Blackburn eventually began to tire and play less effectively. It also became clear that Richter's difficulty with post-concussion syndrome might never abate, and that more help was needed. "We had to make a deal," said Rangers general manager Glen Sather. "I did not want to see Danny lose his confidence and struggle, or for our team to struggle."

Sather traded for Nashville's Mike Dunham, an experienced number-one goaltender, in order to let Blackburn develop at a slower pace. Blackburn finished the season with a 3.17 average and a slightly disappointing .890 save percentage.

The 2003–04 campaign started poorly for Blackburn. Already battling mononucleosis, he attended the Rangers prospects camp to get tuned up early. Unfortunately, he damaged a nerve in his left shoulder and missed training camp and the entire season. There was no panic in New York, though. The three-year veteran was only 20. There were still plenty of games ahead for Dan Blackburn.

	GP	W	L	SO	AVE
RS	63	20	32	1	3.22
PO	0	0	0	0	0

DATE OF BIRTH
Winthrop, Massachusetts
September 19, 1981–

NHL CAREER
2000–01, 2002–04
NY Islanders

Rick DiPietro

Rick DiPietro made history at the 2000 NHL entry draft, and only history will prove whether that was a curse or a blessing. The New York Islanders made DiPietro the first goaltender ever to be picked first overall in the draft.

"We're hanging a lot of reputation on this kid," said Islanders general manager Mike Milbury. "It's gutsy, and maybe crazy, but we think he's a really special player." Before selecting DiPietro, "Mad Mike" dealt the Isles' two top goalies, Kevin Weekes and Roberto Luongo, to open up a spot in the lineup.

The 18-year-old DiPietro had raised a few eyebrows around the league the previous day at a prospects luncheon, talking freely about playing in the NHL as a teenager. "Only a few guys have been able to step right into the NHL, but it's something I hope I can do. If I get the opportunity to step right in, that would be fantastic. I'm optimistic. Some people might call me arrogant or cocky, but I'm just confident. And confidence is a good quality to have for a goalie."

"Some people might call me arrogant or cocky, but I'm just confident."

DiPietro had good reason to be so self-assured. The Lewiston, Maine, native had just completed a standout freshman season with Boston University, winning 17 games, losing 3 and tying 5, with a 2.50 goals-against average and a .909 save percentage. DiPietro set an NCAA record with 77 saves in one game, and was awarded top rookie and Second All-Star Team honors. He also shone for Team USA at the 2000 World Junior Championships, where he earned Top Goaltender status.

DiPietro's puckhandling skills already rivaled those of many NHL netminders. "We've had some good goaltenders here, but no one moves the puck like he does," praised Boston U. coach Jack Parker. "What makes that so nice is that he stops it so well too."

At five-foot-eleven and 185 pounds, DiPietro is nimble on his feet. He drops into the butterfly position quickly and recovers well in scrambles. But it's DiPietro's aggressive and competitive nature that takes his game to a higher level. He is a southpaw who catches with a lightning-fast right hand. And DiPietro's been known to offer a little open net, to challenge shooters to beat him snag-side.

DiPietro signed a rich contract for the rookie maximum of almost $1-million per season, with generous incentives, and shortly after his 19th birthday, DiPietro made his first professional start. It was with the Chicago Wolves in the International Hockey League, however, and not with New York.

The last-place Isles didn't call him up for his first NHL start until February 1, 2001. DiPietro only let in a single goal to the Philadelphia Flyers, but still lost the game. By the end of the season, he had a discouraging 3-15-1 record and a disappointing 3.49 goals-against average.

DiPietro spent the 2001–02 campaign with Bridgeport in the American Hockey League. He led the AHL with 30 wins and posted an excellent 2.32 goals-against average. Yet his name swirled in trade rumors. He rejoined the Islanders for the last third of the 2002–03 schedule, and sighed with relief when the club traded his teammate Chris Osgood instead of him.

DiPietro summed up his first three pro seasons with a welcome maturity. "I'd call it going down, taking my medicine and realizing I was young and needed to learn things." When DiPietro entered training camp the following autumn, it was with real appreciation.

"Just being on the team right now this early in the season has been huge," said the 22-year-old goalie. "This year it's been nice to feel a little bit more comfortable around the guys, get to know them, joke around and have a good time, knowing that I was going to be up here from the start." It was the beginning he'd been looking forward to for years. DiPietro notched his first NHL shutout in his first 2003–04 start.

	GP	W	L	SO	AVE
RS	80	28	38	5	2.71
PO	1	0	0	0	0

DATE OF BIRTH
Sorel, Quebec
November 28, 1984–

NHL CAREER
2003–04
Pittsburgh

Marc-Andre Fleury

When Marc-Andre Fleury entered the Pittsburgh Penguins' 2003 training camp, Mario Lemieux invited him to live with him. Lemieux remembered how it felt to arrive alone in the city as a French-Canadian teenager. Would he make Fleury, the number-one pick in the 2003 NHL entry draft, pay rent? "Absolutely," laughed the owner and resident superstar of the Pittsburgh Penguins. "He's got to babysit the kids, too. That's what he did last night."

Lemieux is rumored to have been so impressed by Fleury's skills in the net that he instructed Pittsburgh general manager Craig Patrick to sign Fleury for the 2003–04 season. Publicly, Patrick was non-committal. "There's a lot of factors to weigh," noted Patrick. "The fact that he's 18 years old, the fact that we're not sure what kind of lineup we're going to have yet. That's something we have to discuss, too. And we have to weigh the fact that, if he goes back to Cape Breton, they have a great team. He could learn a lot about winning down there because they should go all the way."

"So far, so great."

League rules stipulate that without a signed contract by October 1, junior-eligible players must return to junior hockey for another season. And if he didn't sign by the summer of 2004, Fleury would be an unrestricted free agent in the spring of 2005.

Patrick, who had traded Pittsburgh's third pick and winger Mikael Samuelsson to Florida to get the Panthers first pick, explained, "We didn't want to make those good moves and have it disappear. It was important to get him signed."

Interestingly, the Penguins already had one of the league's best young goalies under contract. Sebastien Caron played well enough over 24 games in 2002–03 to make the NHL's All-Rookie Team. But the Penguins coveted Fleury for his potential as a franchise cornerstone.

While the Penguins had been on a well-publicized austerity program for some time, trading most of their high-priced talent, Patrick opened the vaults for Fleury. He not only offered the league's maximum rookie salary, but he also matched the generous incentives that the New York Islanders had given their rookie goalie Rick DiPietro in 2000. Potentially, Fleury could more than triple his base salary.

Fleury had completed three stellar seasons with Cape Breton of the Quebec Major Junior Hockey League before the Penguins drafted him. But it was Fleury's dominance at the 2003 World Junior Championships that lifted him into the top position at the NHL draft. Fleury was voted the tournament MVP, having pulled the Canadian side through several difficult games while battling a stomach virus.

"He's a goalie who can make a big difference in a tournament like this and that's what he's done so far," said Canadian assistant coach Mario Durocher. "He's composed with the stress and the pressure…. He's the kind of guy who is smart with good off-ice preparation."

The Russians deservedly won the gold medal, but Fleury kept the deciding game—Russia 3, Canada 2—much closer than the score indicates. He returned to Cape Breton with a silver medal for Canada and the gratitude of a hockey-crazed nation.

While Caron struggled, Fleury got a great start to his NHL career. "So far, so great," said Penguins coach Eddie Olczyk.

"He's been very impressive," agreed Patrick. "Especially his quickness and the way he challenges shooters."

At six-foot-two and 172 pounds, Fleury is a wiry butterfly goalie who plays the angles well. He intentionally keeps a relaxed and playful manner. "I don't like to be too focused and serious, because then I get nervous and I don't like it," he said. "I always admired [Martin] Brodeur, the way he always seems to have fun while he's playing, with a smile. And I like the way he plays because his style is not always a butterfly."

Asked how he would cope facing his role model in a game, Fleury responded wisely, "I will try to not look at the other end."

	GP	W	L	SO	AVE
RS	21	4	14	1	3.64
PO	0	0	0	0	0

DATE OF BIRTH
Montreal, Quebec
April 4, 1979–

NHL CAREER
1999–2004
NY Islanders, Florida

Roberto Luongo

Roberto Luongo began his record-breaking junior hockey career at the age of 16. He joined the Foreurs de Val-d'Or of the Quebec Major Junior Hockey League in 1995–96, and notched a team-record 32 wins in his second season. In 1997–98, Luongo backstopped the Foreurs to the Memorial Cup finals and established a league regular-season record with 7 shutouts. After being traded to Acadie-Bathurst midway through the 1998–99 season, he again went to the Cup finals. But midway through those four successful junior years, the NHL intruded in Luongo's life in a spectacular way.

At the 1997 NHL entry draft, New York Islanders general manager Mike Milbury used the club's first pick, the fourth overall, to choose six-foot-three, 205-pound Luongo. No goaltender had ever been drafted so high. The Isles returned 18-year-old Luongo to his junior club, but they had every intention of dressing him in an NHL sweater in 1998–99. Contractual problems changed the plan.

"I can't score goals, so I can't worry about that and be distracted by it."

"I guess everybody believes because he is a No. 1 pick, he should be playing with us now," Isles director of player personnel Gordie Clark said. "But he wasn't going to beat out Tommy Salo, and sitting on the bench wasn't going to do him any good. We like the experience he has been getting in junior."

He finally signed a contract, but Luongo was bitterly dismayed when the Islanders sent him to the American Hockey League. "When I got here I told myself to just work hard and get some experience," said Luongo during his tenure with the Lowell Lock Monsters. "Just try to get better every day." He finally got his first NHL start with the Islanders on November 28, 1999, stopping 43 pucks during a 2-1 win over Boston.

He tallied a 3.25 goals-against average and .904 save percentage over 24 games with the Islanders, the league's third-worst team, but after helping Lowell in the playoffs, Luongo's days with New York were over.

"We're rolling the dice here a little bit," admitted "Mad Mike" Milbury. "Roberto Luongo is going to be an excellent goaltender in this league. He is a class act and a kid we would have been happy to ride with." But Milbury eclipsed his boldness in drafting Luongo so high by making goalie Rick DiPietro the No.

1 pick in the 2000 NHL entry draft. Clearing the deck for DiPietro, Milbury traded Luongo to the Florida Panthers.

Luongo played 58 games for Florida in 2000–01 and had a sparkling .920 save percentage. Unfortunately, his new club wasn't much better than the Islanders. Partway through another disappointing season in 2001–02, the Panthers hired new coach "Iron Mike" Keenan. Keenan is well known for frequently pulling goaltenders— once even making four goalie changes in one period.

"It's no big deal," says Luongo. "He does it so much that we expect it. When you're sitting on the bench, you have to be ready, just in case." Luongo faced more than 2,000 shots in 2002–03, yet maintained a .918 save percentage. He saw almost 2,500 shots the following season and posted a sparkling .931 save percentage. Still, his coach finds cause for criticism.

"He's played a lot of goal, he's had a good save percentage, he's had to stop a lot of shots," admitted Keenan of Luongo, "but he has to learn how to win like the rest of the team does."

"You can't possibly take that much rubber day in and day out," maintains Edmonton's Eric Brewer, a former Islanders teammate of Luongo's. "After a while—40 shots a game—not only is it wearing your gear, it's wearing your mind." But Luongo remains unflappable and refuses to discuss the Panthers' anemic offense.

"I can't score goals, so I can't worry about that and be distracted by it," says Luongo. "I just worry about what I've got to do and don't try to control anything else. All of this is in the hope of winning a Stanley Cup one day. That's everybody's goal in this dressing room. I don't know how many guys are going to be here when that happens, but hopefully it will be a lot of us."

	GP	W	L	SO	AVE
RS	266	80	138	23	2.64
PO	0	0	0	0	0

DATE OF BIRTH
Belleville, Ontario
May 4, 1980–

NHL CAREER
2000–04
Boston

Andrew Raycroft

"Until the regular season starts and they tell you to go get a place and get settled, I'm still living out of my car and still living at the hotel," said Andrew Raycroft. Boston Bruins general manager Mike O'Connell had just announced that Raycroft and Felix Potvin would start the 2003–04 campaign as the team's top two goalies.

Raycroft's reticence was the logical result of observation and experience. The Bruins had drafted him in 1998, and he'd seen plenty of goalies come and go since then. Still, Bruins management had treated Raycroft with patience. He had a bit of a pedigree and was only getting better.

Boston drafted Raycroft with the 135th pick in the 1998 entry draft, after he had posted a stunning season in junior hockey. Raycroft played two seasons of junior hockey for the Sudbury Wolves of the Ontario Hockey League, then moved to the Kingston Frontenacs for the 1999–2000 campaign. He faced more shots than any other netminder—an average of 41.7 shots per game—but posted a remarkable league-leading .918 save percentage over 61 games. Raycroft was named to the OHL's First All-Star Team and the Canadian Major Junior First All-Star Team. He was named Canadian junior hockey's Goaltender of the Year and also received the OHL's Red Tilson Award for Most Outstanding Player— the first goaltender in 50 years to be so honored.

"I'm still living out of my car."

The first goalie drafted by the Bruins since 1995, Raycroft had a backer in Gerry Cheevers, a Hall of Fame netminder and Boston scout. Cheevers had seen enough one-year wonders to know that a truckload of junior awards meant nothing in the NHL, but he also recognized talent when he saw it. There was work to be done, though. Cheevers didn't play regularly in the NHL until he was almost 26 years old, and he believed in apprenticeship. At six-foot-one and a stringy 150 pounds, Raycroft possessed strong reflexes and a great glove hand, but he needed to develop more strength to withstand the rigors of the professional game.

With Byron Dafoe recovering from knee surgery, Raycroft was pushed into action with the Bruins at the start of the 2000–01 season. At 20 years old, he became the youngest goaltender to win a game in a Boston uniform since 19-year-old Bill Ranford won on March 29, 1986. Raycroft played in 15 games before being sent to the Providence Bruins in the American Hockey League.

In 2001–02, Raycroft took over the starting role in Providence, amassing a strong 2.57 goals-against average and a .916 save percentage over 56 games. Boston called him up for one relief effort, and he backstopped the Bruins to a 3-3 tie against the New York Islanders before returning to Providence. Raycroft posted another strong AHL campaign in 2002–03, winning 23 games, losing 10 and tying 3, with a 2.50 goals-against average and a .917 save percentage. He had almost identical percentages in five NHL appearances with the parent club. Technically sound, and with his weight up around 170 pounds, Raycroft was ready for bigger challenges.

"Andrew is one of our brightest young players," said O'Connell in July 2003. "He has certainly proven himself at the AHL level over the last couple of seasons and has played well in Boston when the need arose. We certainly expect that he will challenge for the number-one goaltending position in training camp this fall."

As promised, Raycroft got his share of starts early in 2003–04. He notched his first NHL shutout and Boston's first win of the season on October 15, 2003, against the Dallas Stars. By mid-season, he had played twice as much as Potvin, and possessed one of the league's best save percentages.

"There was no doubt in my mind that he could come in here and do the same thing he did in Providence," praised Boston's new coach Mike Sullivan. "He worked real hard in the summertime and has taken control of his game." Likewise, Boston has perhaps taken care of its goaltending for years to come. Raycroft's play lifted the Bruins into the playoffs, and at the season's end he was awarded the Calder Trophy as rookie of the year.

	GP	W	L	SO	AVE	AWARDS
RS	78	35	27	3	2.22	Calder
PO	7	3	4	1	2.14	

NOTES ON THE PHOTOGRAPHS

front cover: Bruce Bennett Studios/Getty Images

back cover: (top left) Ken Levine/Getty Images; (top middle) Bruce Bennett Studios/Getty Images; (top right) Elsa/Allsport/Getty Images; (bottom): Bruce Bennett/Getty Images

p. 2-3 Steve Yzerman and Patrick Roy; Red Wings vs. Avalanche; May 29, 2002; Elsa/Getty Images/NHLI

p. 4 Maurice Richard; Canadiens vs. Black Hawks; 1952; Hy Peskin//Time Life Pictures/Getty Images

p. 8 Beliveau - Geoffrion;Imperial Oil-Turofsky/Hockey Hall of Fame

p. 10 Joe Thornton and Jose Theodore; Canadiens vs. Bruins; April 17, 2004; Charles Laberge/Getty Images

p. 12-13 Wayne Gretzky and Bryan Trottier; Oilers vs. Islanders; circa 1970s; Focus on Sport/Getty Images

p. 14 Scott Gomez; Devils vs. Mighty Ducks; June 9, 2003; Dave Sandford/Getty Images/NHLI

p. 16 Syl Apps; circa 1940s; Bruce Bennett Studios/Getty Images

p. 17 Syl Apps; Toronto Maple Leafs; April 16, 1948; Bruce Bennett Studios/Getty Images

p. 18 Jean Beliveau; Canadiens vs. Blackhawks; May 1, 1965; Bruce Bennett Studios/Getty Images

p. 19 Jean Beliveau; Bruins vs. Canadiens; March 11, 1956; Bruce Bennett Studios/Getty Images

p. 20 Bobby Clarke; Philadelphia Flyers; early 1980s, Bruce Bennett Studios/Getty Images

p. 21 Bobby Clarke; Flyers vs. Islanders; circa 1970s ; Bruce Bennett Studios/Getty Images

p. 22 Marcel Dionne; Detroit Red Wings; January 1975; Bruce Bennett Studios/Getty Images

p. 23 Marcel Dionne; Kings vs. Islanders; early 1980s; Bruce Bennett Studios/Getty Images

p. 24 Phil Esposito; New York Rangers; circa 1979; Focus on Sport/Getty Images

p. 25 Phil Esposito; Bruins vs. Rangers; circa 1970s; Melchior DiGiacomo/Getty Images

p. 26 Wayne Gretzky; Edmonton Oilers; mid 1980s; Bruce Bennett/Getty Images

p. 27 Wayne Gretzky; Rangers vs. Sabres; December 13, 1996; Rick Stewart/Stringer/Getty Images

p. 28 Mario Lemieux; Penguins vs. Mighty Ducks; December 15, 2002; Donald Miralle/Getty Images

p. 29 Mario Lemieux; Penguins vs. Islanders; early 1990s; Bruce Bennett Studios/Getty Images

p. 31 Mark Messier; Oilers vs. Flyers; 1987; Bruce Bennett Studios/Getty Images

p. 32 Stan Mikita; Black Hawks vs. Maple Leafs; 1960s; Bruce Bennett Studios/Getty Images

p. 33 Stan Mikita; Black Hawks vs. North Stars; Focus on Sport/Getty Images

p. 34 Howie Morenz; 1930s; Bruce Bennett Studios/Getty Images

p. 35 Howie Morenz; Canadiens vs. Rangers; Hockey Hall of Fame

p. 36 Henri Richard; 1960s; Bruce Bennett Studios/Getty Images

p. 37 Henri Richard; Montreal Canadiens; early 1970s; Melchior DiGiacomo/Getty Images

p. 38 Milt Schmidt; Boston Bruins; mid 20th century; Bruce Bennett Studios/Getty Images

p. 39 Milt Schmidt; Bruins vs. Rangers; January 17, 1946; Bruce Bennett Studios/Getty Images

p. 41 Nels Stewart; 1920s; Bruce Bennett Studios/Getty Images

p. 42 Bryan Trottier; Penguins vs. Sabres; January 7, 1994; Rick Stewart/Getty Images

p. 43 Bryan Trottier; Islanders vs. Devils; late 1980s; Bruce Bennett Studios/Getty Images

p. 45 Steve Yzerman; Red Wings vs. Predators; April 11, 2004; Brian Bahr/Getty Images

p. 46 Mike Comrie; Coyotes vs. Predators; February 21, 2004; Barry Gossage/Getty Images

p. 48 Scott Gomez; Devils vs. Panthers; November 13, 2003; Al Bello/Getty Images

p. 50 Vincent Lecavalier; Lightning vs. Canadiens; April 27, 2004; Dave Sandford/Getty Images

p. 52 Jason Spezza; Senators vs. Maple Leafs; January 8, 2004; Dave Sandford/Getty Images

p. 54 Joe Thornton; Bruins vs. Canadiens; April 17, 2004; Charles Laberge/Getty Images

p. 56-57 Mats Sundin (right) and Ilya Kovalchuk; Maple Leafs vs. Thrashers; October 27, 2003; Dave Sandford/Getty Images

p. 58 Maurice Richard and Dickie Moore; Imperial Oil-Turofsky/Hockey Hall of Fame

p. 60 Mike Bossy; New York Islanders; 1980s; Bruce Bennett Studios/Getty Images

p. 61 Mike Bossy; New York Islanders; 1980s; Bruce Bennett Studios/Getty Images

p. 62 Johnny Bucyk; Bruins vs. Flyers; 1970s; Melchior DiGiacomo/Getty Images

p. 63 Johnny Bucyk; Boston Bruins; 1970s; Bruce Bennett Studios/Getty Images

p. 65 Charlie Conacher; 1933; Bruce Bennett Studios/Getty Images

p. 66 Mike Gartner; Maple Leafs vs. Canadiens; mid 1990s; Robert Laberge/Getty Images

p. 67 Mike Gartner; Capitols vs. Islanders; 1980s; Bruce Bennett Studios/Getty Images

p. 68 Bernie Geoffrion; Montreal Canadiens; 1960s; Bruce Bennett Studios/Getty Images

p. 69 Bernie Geoffrion; late 1960s; Bruce Bennett Studios/Getty Images

p. 70 Gordie Howe; Hartford Whalers; circa 1980; Focus on Sport/Getty Images

p. 71 Gordie Howe; Red Wings vs. Rangers; Stan Wayman//Time Life Pictures/Getty Images

p. 72 Bobby Hull; Blackhawks vs. Rangers; Bill Eppridge/Time Life Pictures/Getty Images

p. 73 Bobby Hull; Blackhawks vs. Rangers; 1970s; Melchior DiGiacomo/Getty Images

p. 74 Brett Hull; Red Wings vs. Maple Leafs; December 6, 2003; Dave Sandford/Getty Images

p. 75 Brett Hull; Blues vs. Rangers; early 1990s; Bruce Bennett Studios/Getty Images

p. 76 Jaromir Jagr; Penguins vs. North Stars; 1991; Bruce Bennett Studios/Getty Images

p. 77 Jaromir Jagr; Rangers vs. Panthers; January 26, 2004; Ezra Shaw/Getty Images

p. 78 Jari Kurri; Kings vs. Canadiens; 1994; Robert Laberge/ALLSPORT/Getty Images

p. 79 Jari Kurri; Oilers vs. Blues; 1980s; Bruce Bennett Studios/Getty Images

p. 80 Guy Lafleur; Montreal Canadiens; late 1970s or early 1980s; Bruce Bennett Studios/Getty Images

p. 81 Guy Lafleur; Nordiques vs. Sabres; 1990; Rick Stewart/Getty Images

p. 82 Ted Lindsay; Detroit Red Wings; 1954; Bruce Bennett Studios/Getty Images

p. 83 Ted Lindsay (center, in white); Red Wings vs. Maple Leafs; October 14, 1951; Bruce Bennett Studios/Getty Images

p. 84 Frank Mahovlich; Toronto Maple Leafs; March 21, 1965; Pictorial Parade/Getty Images

p. 85 Frank Mahovlich; Canadiens vs. Rangers; 1970s; Melchior DiGiacomo/Getty Images

p. 87 Dickie Moore; early 1950s; Bruce Bennett Studios/Getty Images

p. 89 Maurice Richard; Montreal Canadiens; circa 1942; Bruce Bennett Studios/Getty Images

p. 90 Marian Gaborik; Wild vs. Kings; March 4, 2004; Robert Laberge/Getty Images

p. 92 Dany Heatley; Thrashers vs. Rangers; 2003; Bruce Bennett Studios/Getty Images

p. 94 Marian Hossa; Senators vs. Maple Leafs; April 12, 2004; Dave Sandford/Getty Images

p. 96 Ilya Kovalchuk; Thrashers vs. Panthers; March 19, 2004; Scott Cunningham/Getty Images

p. 98 Henrik Zetterberg; Red Wings vs. Blues; April 1, 2004; Elsa/Getty Images

p. 100-101 Billy Smith (#31); Islanders vs. Bruins; Anthony Neste/Time Life Pictures/Getty Images

p. 102 Tim Horton (#2), Jim Schoenfeld (#6), Roger Crozier (#1), and Paul Henderson (#19); Sabres vs. Maple Leafs; early 1970s; Melchior DiGiacomo/Getty Images

p. 104 Ray Bourque; Avalanche vs. Devils; June 9, 2001; Elsa/Allsport/Getty Images

p. 105 Ray Bourque; Bruins vs. Devils; circa 1990s; Bruce Bennet Studios/Getty Images

p. 106 Chris Chelios; Blackhawks vs. Flames; January 28, 1999; Ian Tomlinson /Allsport/Getty Images

p. 107 Chris Chelios; Red Wings vs. Blues; December 4, 2003; Elsa/Getty Images

p. 109 King Clancy; Imperial Oil-Turofsky/Hockey Hall of Fame

p. 111 Dit Clapper; 1930s; Bruce Bennett Studios/Getty Images

p. 112 Paul Coffey; Red Wings vs. Maple Leafs; circa 1995; Claus Andersen/Bruce Bennett Studios/Getty Images

p. 113 Paul Coffey; Edmonton Oilers; mid 1980s; Bruce Bennett/Getty Images

p. 114 Doug Harvey; Montreal Canadiens; 1950s; Pictorial Parade/Getty Images

p. 115 Doug Harvey; Imperial Oil-Turofsky/Hockey Hall of Fame

p. 116 Tim Horton; Maple Leafs vs. Canadiens; February 1, 1967; Bruce Bennett Studios/Getty Images

p. 117 Tim Horton; Maple Leafs vs. Bruins; 1960s; Bruce Bennett Studios/Getty Images

p. 118 Red Kelly; 1960s; Bruce Bennett Studios/Getty Images

p. 119 Red Kelly; Red Wings vs. Canadiens; April 16, 1954; Bruce Bennett Studios/Getty Images

p. 120 Bobby Orr; Boston Bruins; 1970s; Melchior DiGiacomo/Getty Images

p. 121 Bobby Orr; Boston Bruins; 1970s; Melchior DiGiacomo/Getty Images

p. 122 Brad Park; Boston Bruins; 1970s; Bruce Bennett Studios/Getty Images

p. 123 Brad Park; Rangers vs. Red Wings; January 1974; Bruce Bennett Studios/Getty Images

p. 124 Pierre Pilote; Norris Trophy for the NHL's Outstanding Defenseman; 1964; Bruce Bennett Studios/Getty Images

p. 125 Pierre Pilote; Black Hawks vs. North Stars; March 17, 1968; Bruce Bennett Studios/Getty Images

p. 126 Denis Potvin; Islanders vs. Oilers; 1980s; Bruce Bennett Studios/Getty Images

p. 127 Denis Potvin; New York Islanders; 1980s; Bruce Bennett Studios/Getty Images

p. 128 Larry Robinson; Kings vs. Jets; Ken Levine/Getty Images

p. 129 Larry Robinson; Montreal Canadiens; late 1970s; Bruce Bennett Studios/Getty Images

p. 130 Serge Savard; Canadiens vs. Rangers; circa 1979; Focus on Sport/Getty Images

p. 131 Serge Savard; Canadiens vs. Rangers; 1970s; Melchior DiGiacomo/Getty Images

p. 132 Eddie Shore; January 28, 1934; FPG/Getty Images

p. 133 Eddie Shore; 1939; Bruce Bennett Studios/Getty Images

p. 134 Jay Bouwmeester; Panthers vs. Stars; December 19, 2003; Eliot J. Schechter/Getty Images

p. 136 Eric Brewer; Oilers vs. Avalanche; October 23, 2003; Brian Bahr/Getty Images

p. 138 Jiri Fischer; Red Wings vs. Hurricanes; June 10, 2002; Craig Jones/Getty Images/NHLI

p. 140 Barret Jackman; St Louis Blues; 2003; Bruce Bennett Studios/Getty Images

p. 142 Robyn Regehr; Flames vs. Lightning; June 7, 2004; Jeff Gross/Getty Images

p. 144-145 Dominik Hasek; Detroit Red Wings; 2004; Bruce Bennett Studios/Getty Images

p. 146 Jacques Plante; Imperial Oil-Turofsky/Hockey Hall of Fame

p. 148 Johnny Bower; Maple Leafs vs. Bruins; February 23, 1963; Bruce Bennett Studios/Getty Images

p. 149 Johnny Bower; Toronto Maple Leafs; 1960s; Pictorial Parade/Hulton Archive/Getty Images

p. 151 Frank Brimsek; Bruins vs. Rangers; October 31, 1948; Bruce Bennett Studios/Getty Images

p. 152 Turk Broda; 1940s; Bruce Bennett Studios/Getty Images

p. 153 Turk Broda; Toronto Maple Leafs; December 22, 1946; Bruce Bennett Studios/Getty Images

p. 154 Ken Dryden; Montreal Canadiens; 1970s; Bruce Bennett Studios/Getty Images

p. 155 Ken Dryden; Montreal Canadiens; 1970s; Bruce Bennett Studios/Getty Images

p. 157 Bill Durnan; Imperial Oil-Turofsky/Hockey Hall of Fame

p. 158 Grant Fuhr; Oilers vs. Flyers; 1987; Bruce Bennett StudiosGetty Images

p. 159 Grant Fuhr; Edmonton Oilers; 1980s; Bruce Bennett Studios/Getty Images

p. 160 Glenn Hall; Blues vs. Canadiens; December 4, 1970; Bruce Bennett Studios/Getty Images

p. 161 Glenn Hall; Chicago Black Hawks; Francis Miller/Time Life Pictures/Getty Images

p. 163 Dominik Hasek; Red Wings vs. Avalanche; May 27, 2002; Dave Sandford/Getty Images/NHLI

p. 165 Bernie Parent; London-Life-Portnoy/Hockey Hall of Fame

p. 166 Jacques Plante; Montreal Canadiens; September 30, 1960; Pictorial Parade/Getty Images

p. 167 Jacques Plante; Canadiens vs. Rangers; February 27, 1955; Bruce Bennett Studios/Getty Images

p. 168 Patrick Roy; Montreal Canadiens; 1989-1990; Ken Levine /Allsport/Getty Images

p. 169 Patrick Roy; Avalanche vs. Wild; April 22, 2003; Brian Bahr/Getty Images/NHLI

p. 170 Terry Sawchuk; Red Wings vs. Canadiens; 1950s; Pictorial Parade/Getty Images

p. 171 Terry Sawchuk; Detroit Red Wings; 1950s; Joseph Scherschel//Time Life Pictures/Getty Images

p. 172 Billy Smith; Islanders vs. North Stars; circa 1981; Focus on Sport/Getty Images

p. 173 Billy Smith; New York Islanders; 1980s; Bruce Bennett Studios/Getty Images

p. 174 Vladislav Tretiak, early 1980s, Bruce Bennett Studios/Getty Images

p. 175 Vladislav Tretiak; 1980; Bruce Bennett Studios/Getty Images

p. 176 Lorne 'Gump' Worsley; Canadiens vs. Seals; November 18, 1967; Bruce Bennett Studios/Getty Images

p. 177 Lorne 'Gump' Worsley; New York Rangers; 1950s; Pictorial Parade/Getty Images

p. 178 Dan Blackburn; Rangers vs. Blues; February 6, 2003; Elsa/Getty Images/NHLI

p. 180 Rick DiPietro; Islanders vs. Bruins; January 27, 2004; Al Bello/Getty Images

p. 182 Marc-Andre Fleury; Penguins vs. Senators; January 22, 2004; Dave Sandford/Getty Images

p. 184 Roberto Luongo; Panthers vs. Devils; October 22, 2003; Al Bello/Getty Images

p. 186 Andrew Raycroft; Bruins vs. Canadiens; April 7, 2004; Elsa/Getty Images

BIBLIOGRAPHY

The books listed here were of immeasurable assistance, but several other sources were equally useful. The archived newspaper and magazine clippings at the Hockey Hall of Fame in Toronto as well as the Hall web site (www.hhof.com) provided a wealth of material. Other internet sites I frequently visited are run by the *Sun* newspaper chain (www.canoe.com/Hockey/home.html); ESPN (ESPNET.SportsZone.com/nhl); and *LCS Guide to Hockey*. (www.lcshockey.com), written by Joe Pelletier and Pat Houda. Dozens of other web sites — primarily run by fans out of an enthusiastic loyalty to the game and particular players — were of some practical use. Many newspaper web sites, especially those of *The Boston Globe, The St. Louis Post-Dispatch, The London Free Press, The Toronto Star*, and *The Globe and Mail* were also helpful.

Dozens of issues of *The Hockey News* were used as sources, and their numerous writers and editors deserve credit, not only from me, for the fine work they do for the sport of hockey. Articles in *Sports Illustrated* were also useful. Several editions of the annual *National Hockey League Official Guide and Record Book* and both volumes of *Total Hockey: The Official Encyclopedial of the National Hockey League* were indispensable for their statistical information, as were a large assortment of individual clubs' NHL media guides.

Benedict, Michael, and D'Arcy Jenish, eds. *Canada On Ice: Fifty Years of Great Hockey*. Toronto: The Penguin Group, 1998.

Brewitt, Ross. *Last Minute of Play: Tales of Hockey Grit and Glory*. Toronto: Stoddart Publishing Co. Ltd., 1993.

Dryden, Steve, ed. *The Top 100: NHL Players of All Time*. Toronto: McClelland & Stewart Inc., 1998.

Fischler, Stan. *Bad Boys: The Legends of Hockey's Toughest, Meanest, Most-Feared Players*. Whitby: McGraw-Hill Ryerson Ltd, 1991.

-------- . *Bobby Orr and the Big, Bad Bruins*. New York: Dell Publishing Co., Inc., 1969.

-------- . *Golden Ice: The Greatest Teams in Hockey History*. Scarborough: McGraw-Hill Ryerson Ltd., 1990.

-------- . *The Rivalry: Canadiens vs Leafs*. Whitby: McGraw-Hill Ryerson Ltd, 1991.

Goyens, Chris and Allan Turowetz. *Lions in Winter*. Scarborough: Prentice-Hall Canada Inc., 1986.

Houston, William. *Pride & Glory: 100 Years of the Stanley Cup*. Whitby: McGraw-Hill Ryerson Ltd., 1992.

Hughes, Morgan. *Best of Hockey*. Chicago: Publications International, Inc., 1998.

-------- . *Hockey Legends of All Time*. Chicago: Publications International, Inc., 1996.

Hunter, Douglas. *A Breed Apart: An Illustrated History of Goaltending*. Toronto: Viking, 1995.

-------- . Champions: *The Illustrated History of Hockey's Greatest Dynasties*. Toronto: Penguin Studio, 1997.

-------- . *Open Ice: The Tim Horton Story*. Toronto: Viking, 1997.

Irvin, Dick. *The Habs: An Oral History of the Montreal Canadiens, 1940-1980*. Toronto: McClelland & Stewart, 1991.

Klein, Jeff Z. and Karl-Eric Reif. *The Coolest Guys on Ice*. Atlanta: Turner Publishing, Inc., 1996.

Leonetti, Mike. *Hockey's Golden Era: Stars of the Original Six*. Toronto: Macmillan of Canada, 1993.

MacGregor, Roy. *The Home Team: Fathers, Sons & Hockey*. Toronto: Viking, 1995.

McKinley, Michael. *Hockey Hall of Fame Legends*. Toronto: Viking/Opus Productions, 1993.

Potvin, Denis with Stan Fischler. *Power On Ice*. New York, Harper & Row, 1977.

Robinson, Larry and Chris Goyens. *Robinson For the Defence*. Scarborough: McGraw-Hill Ryerson Ltd., 1988.

Romain, Joseph and James Duplacey. *Hockey Superstars*. Toronto: Smithbooks in Canada, 1994.

Roxborough, Henry. *The Stanley Cup Story*. Toronto: The Ryerson Press, 1964.

INDEX

A two-page spread indicates the main entry for a player. **Boldface** type indicates other photographs in which the player appears.

Abel, Sid, 70, 82, 118
Adams, Jack, 62, 70, 118, 147, 160
Apps, Syl, 16–17
Arbour, Al, 126

Bailey, Ace, 132
Ballard, Harold, 116
Bathgate, Andy, 68, 84, 166
Bauer, Bobby, 38
Belfour, Eddie, 162, 174
Beliveau, Jean, **8**, 18–19, 36, 40, 68
Benedict, Clint, 108
Berard, Bryan, 95
Blackburn, Dan, 178–79
Blair, Wren, 176
Blake, Hector "Toe," 36, 86, 166, 176
Boivin, Leo, 126
Bondra, Peter, 66
Bossy, Mike, 42, 59, 60–61, 88
Bouchard, Emile "Butch," 38
Bourque, Raymond, 103, 104–5
Bouwmeester, Jay, 134–35
Bower, Johnny, **58**, 72, 148–49, 170, 176
Bowman, Scotty, 44, 154
Brewer, Eric, 136–37
Brimsek, Frank, 150–51
Broda, Walter "Turk," 152–53
Brodeur, Martin, 183
Bucyk, Johnny, 59, 62–63
Bure, Pavel, 10
Burns, Pat, 49
Button, Craig, 143

Calder, Frank, 108
Campbell, Clarence, 88, 110
Caron, Sebastien, 183
Carter, Anson, 47
Chadwick, Ed, 148
Chara, Zdeno, 53
Cheevers, Gerry, 187
Chelios, Chris, 103, 106–7, 139
Chelios, Gus, 106
Cherry, Don, 122
Clancy, Francis "King," 64, 103, 108–9, 118
Clapper, Aubrey "Dit," 110–11, 150

Clarke, Bobby, 20–21, 47
Coffey, Paul, 103, 112–13
Comrie, Mike, 46–47
Conacher, Charlie, 64–65, 68
Conacher, Lionel, 64
Conacher, Pete, 64
Conacher, Roy, 64
Cook, Frederick "Bun," 34
Corbeau, Bert, 40
Coutu, Billy, 132
Cowley, Bill, 110
Crozier, Roger, **102**, 176

Dafoe, Byron, 187
Dandurand, Leo, 34
Datsyuk, Pavel, 99
Davidson, John, 179
Day, Clarence "Hap," 68
Delvecchio, Alex, 84
Demers, Jacques, 44
Demitra, Pavol, 95
Dionne, Marcel, 10, 15, 22–23, 26
DiPietro, Rick, 180–81, 183, 185
Dryden, Dave, 154
Dryden, Ken, 154–55
Dumart, Woody, 38
Dunham, Mike, 179
Durnan, Bill, 156–57

Eagleson, Alan, 120
Eddolls, Frank, 124
Elias, Patrik, 49
Emms, Leighton "Hap," 164
Esposito, Phil, 15, 24–25, 38, 104, 122
Esposito, Tony, 10, 147, 176

Faulkner, Steve, 156
Favell, Doug, 164
Feaster, Jay, 51
Fedorov, Sergei, 99
Ferguson, John, 130
Fischer, Jiri, 138–39
Fleury, Marc-Andre, 182–83
Francis, Emile, 122
Francis, Ron, 76
Fraser, Curt, 97, 172
Fuhr, Grant, 147, 158–59

Gaborik, Marian, 90–91, 95
Gadsby, Bill, 116
Gallivan, Danny, 130
Gartner, Mike, 10, 66–67

Geoffrion, Bernie "Boom Boom," **8**, 68–69
Gilbert, Greg, 143
Gillies, Clark, 60
Gomez, Scott, **14**, 48–49
Gratton, Chris, 51
Green, Josh, 137
Gretzky, Wayne, 9, 11, **12–13**, 15, 26–27, 70, 78

Hall, Glenn, 82, 147, 160–61, 166, 170, 176
Hamrlik, Roman, 137
Hart, Cecil, 34
Harvey, Doug, 103, 104, 114–15
Hasek, Dominik, **144–45**, 158, 162–63, 174
Hatcher, Derian, 139
Heatley, Dany, 92–93, 97
Hedberg, Anders, 72
Henderson, Paul, 10, 174
Hitchman, Lionel, 110
Hodge, Charlie, 176
Hodge, Ken, 24, 38
Horner, Reginald "Red," 132
Horton, Tim, **102**, 116–17
Horvath, Bronco, 62
Hossa, Marcel, 95
Hossa, Marian, 94–95
Howe, Gordie, 9, 59, 70–71, 82, 84, 110
Howe, Mark, 70
Howe, Marty, 70
Howell, Harry, 103, 122
Hull, Bobby, 24, 32, 59, 72–73, 116
Hull, Brett, 59, 74–75, 99

Iginla, Jarome, 143
Imlach, George "Punch," 84, 116, 148

Jackman, Barret, 99, 135, 140–41
Jackson, Harvey "Busher," 64
Jagr, Jaromir, 59, 76–77
Johnson, Marshall, 53

Keenan, Mike, 55, 74, 135, 158, 185
Kelly, Leonard "Red," **8**, 103, 116, 118–19
Kennedy, Ted, 70
Kharlamov, Valeri, 20, 97
Kiszka, Frank, 106
Kovalchuk, Ilya, **56–57**, 93, 96–97
Kurri, Jari, 59, 78–79

INDEX

Lafleur, Guy, 10, 22, 80–81, 128
Langway, Rod, 103
Lapointe, Guy, 128, 130
Larionov, Igor, 99
Leach, Reggie, 78
Lecavalier, Vincent, 50–51
Lehtonen, Kari, 135
Lemaire, Jacques, 80, 91
Lemieux, Mario, 9, 15, 28–29, 76, 112, 183
Lewis, Dave, 99, 139
Linden, Trevor, 162
Lindros, Eric, 76
Lindsay, Ted, 59, 70, 82–83, 114, 118, 160
Lowe, Kevin, 47
Lumley, Harry, 170
Luongo, Roberto, 181, 184–85
Lydman, Toni, 143

MacInnis, Al, 141
MacNeil, Al, 36
Mahovlich, Frank, 84–85, 112, 118
Marotte, Gilles, 24
Martin, Hubert "Pit," 24
Martin, Jacques, 53, 95
Martin, Rick, 60
McDonald, Wilfred "Bucko," 120
McNeil, Gerry, 156
Melanson, Roland, 172
Messier, Mark, 15, 30–31, 78
Mikita, Stan, 24, 32–33, 72
Milbury, Mike, 137, 181, 185
Mohns, Doug, 32
Moog, Andy, 158
Moore, Dickie, 36, 58, 86–87
Morenz, Howie, 9, 34–35
Muckalt, Bill, 53
Murphy, Larry, 66

Nash, Rick, 135
Nighbor, Frank, 108
Nilsson, Ulf, 72
Norris, Jack, 24

Oates, Adam, 74
O'Connell, Mike, 187
Orr, Bobby, 20, 103, 120–21, 122, 126
Orr, Doug, 120
Osgood, Chris, 181
Ozolinsh, Sandis, 135

Palffy, Zigmund, 95
Parent, Bernie, 164–65
Park, Brad, 24, 103, 122–23
Patrick, Craig, 183
Patrick, Lynn, 38
Picard, Noel, 120
Pilote, Pierre, 103, 120, 124–25
Plante, Jacques, 146, 147, 160, 164, 166–67, 174
Pocklington, Peter, 112
Pollock, Sam, 128
Potvin, Denis, 100–101, 103, 126–27
Potvin, Felix, 158, 187
Pratt, Walter "Babe," 124
Primeau, Joe, 64
Pronger, Chris, 141

Quenneville, Joel, 141

Ramage, Rob, 172
Ranford, Bill, 158, 187
Ratelle, Jean, 24, 122
Raycroft, Andrew, 186–87
Rayner, Chuck, 148, 176
Regehr, Robyn, 142–43
Resch, Glenn "Chico," 172
Richard, Henri, 15, 36–37, 86
Richard, Maurice "Rocket," 4, 9, 11, 36, 58, 59, 68, 86, 88–89
Richards, Brad, 51
Richter, Mike, 179
Risebrough, Doug, 91
Robinson, Larry, 128–29, 130
Rollins, Al, 4, 152
Ross, Art, 110, 151
Roy, Patrick, 162, 168–69
Ruel, Claude, 176

St. Louis, Martin, 51
Sakic, Joe, 104
Salo, Tommy, 185
Samsanov, Sergei, 55
Samuelsson, Mikael, 183
Sanderson, Derek, 116, 120
Satan, Miroslav, 95
Sather, Glen, 112, 179
Savard, Denis, 106
Savard, Serge, 128, 130–31
Sawchuk, Terry, 148, 160, 170–71
Schmidt, Milt, 38–39
Schoenfeld, Jim, 102
Sedin, Daniel, 139

Selanne, Teemu, 49
Selke, Frank, Sr., 118
Shanahan, Brendan, 9, 99
Shore, Eddie, 103, 108, 110, 132–33
Shultz, Dave, 128
Siebert, Albert "Babe," 40
Simmer, Charlie, 22
Simmons, Don, 132
Sinden, Harry, 24, 120
Smith, Billy, 100–101, 172–73
Smith, Reginald "Hooley," 40
Smythe, Conn, 16, 64, 82, 108, 152
Snyder, Dan, 93, 97
Spezza, Jason, 52–53
Stanfield, Fred, 24, 38
Stasiuk, Vic, 62
Stewart, Jack, 38
Stewart, Nels, 9, 15, 40–41, 88
Sundin, Mats, 56–57
Sutter, Brian, 143
Sutter, Duane, 143

Taylor, Dave, 22
Theodore, Jose, 10
Thompson, Cecil "Tiny," 150
Thornton, Joe, 10, 54–55
Tortorella, John, 51
Tremblay, Mario, 168
Tretiak, Vladislav, 10, 174–75
Trottier, Bryan, 12–13, 42–43, 45, 60

Vachon, Rogatien, 176
Vadnais, Carol, 24, 122
Vezina, Georges, 9

Watson, Harry, 16
Weekes, Kevin, 181
Weight, Doug, 47
Westlund, Tommy, 139
Wharram, Ken, 32
Whitney, Ray, 99
Williams, Art, 51
Worsley, Lorne "Gump," 72, 147, 148, 166, 176–77

Yashin, Alexei, 53
Yzerman, Steve, 9, 15, 44–45, 99

Zanussi, Joe, 24, 122
Zetterberg, Henrik, 98–99